To the Sun

To the Sun

by
Guy de Maupassant

translated and edited by James Wilson

Duchy of Lambeth
41 Elmcourt Road
Lambeth
London SE27 9BX

—
2008

All rights reserved. No part of this publication may be reproduced, stored in a retrieval system, or transmitted, in any form or by any means, without the prior permission in writing of Duchy of Lambeth, or as expressly permitted by law, or under terms agreed with the appropriate reprographics rights organization. Enquiries concerning reproduction outside the scope of the above should be sent to Duchy of Lambeth, at the address below. The author's moral rights have been asserted.

Published by:
Duchy of Lambeth
41 Elmcourt Road
Lambeth
London SE27 9BX

Introduction, Select Bibliography, Chronology, Note to the Text, Translation, Notes, Appendix © 2008 James Wilson
Au Soleil first published in French in 1884 (Paris: Victor Havard)

Cover artwork: © James Wilson
Book design: James Wilson

Typeset in the Duchy of Lambeth by the Duke
Printed and bound by Lulu.com

ISBN 978-0-9558525-0-3
British Library Cataloguing-in-Publication Data
A catalogue record for this book is available
from the British Library

Acknowledgements

I would like to thank my parents and all my friends and family for their support. Shout outs in particular to Stephen McNeilly for his design template and guidance in matters of typesetting and production; Ian Brinton at *The Use of English*, who published the first four chapters of this translation; and Rick Wilson for his helpful comments and suggestions. Thanks also to Thierry Selva and his website <http://maupassant.free.fr> which has the vast majority of Maupassant's texts online in French and some in translation too; and to Noëlle Benhamou and her site <http://www. maupassantiana.fr> which has an excellent bibliography and is the best place to keep up to date with all things Maupassant.

JW, 2008

Table of Contents

Introduction *James Wilson*..ix
Select Bibliography..xix
Chronology of Maupassant's Life and Works..................................xxvii
Note to the Text..xxxiii

To the Sun

Chapter One...5
Chapter Two—The Sea..9
Chapter Three—Algiers...11
Chapter Four—The Province of Oran..15
Chapter Five—Bou-Amama...23
Chapter Six—The Province of Algiers..29
Chapter Seven—The Zar'ez..43
Chapter Eight—Kabylie - Bougie..75
Chapter Nine—Constantine..89

Fragments

At the Spas..95
In Brittany...105
Le Creusot...121

Notes..129
Appendix—Place Names in *To the Sun*..155
Index..159

Introduction *James Wilson*

> I have seen lots of camel carcasses, a few Spaniards' skulls, jackals, vipers and vultures.
>
> I have crossed an abominable region in [temperatures of] fifty-six degrees in the shade. I know the great white despair of the desert.
>
> I have burnt my fingers on the barrel of my gun. I have breathed in the sirocco, drunk brackish water, slept with bugs in the midst of grunting beasts; and all this to convince myself one more time of the definitive mindlessness of man. That's all.
>
> Letter to Gisèle d'Estoc [1]

So wrote Guy de Maupassant, returning to Algiers in late July or early August 1881 from a fortnight's journey around the hauts plateaux. Yet for him this was not a form of torture, but a sort of absolution. The 'mindlessness of man' is not here an insult, but almost a compliment, a desired state. The vagabond mode of living, the harsh terrain and even harsher climate made Algeria so attractive to Maupassant precisely because of this ability to destroy thoughts and feelings and nullify the mind. Returning to a primitive, bestial condition was a relief for Maupassant—an escape from and stripping away of the airs and graces of Parisian salons that were ridden with hypocrisy and, for Maupassant, worn with great discomfort, like a pair of ill-fitting shoes.

On July 6, 1881, Maupassant left Paris for Algeria, commissioned by Arthur Meyer, editor of *Le Gaulois*, to go to the troubled colony as the newspaper's correspondent. By this time, Maupassant, approaching his thirty-first birthday, had already established himself as a writer and literary figure with the publication of 'Boule de suif' in *Les Soirées de Médan* the previous year and with his own collection of short stories *La Maison Tellier*, just published by Victor Havard. Maupassant had taken extended leave without pay from his job as a civil servant at the Ministry of Education and for the remainder of his life would live by his pen. It was the beginning of a ten-year period that would see a prodigious output of work: Over 300 short stories, 6 novels, 3 books of travel writing, as well as his journalism, drama, poetry, and correspondence. Maupassant claimed that he only wrote to make money and that he was an *'industriel des lettres'* [industrialist of literature] ² and one of the most profitable goods lines from his factory of words was his journalism. He wrote over two hundred and fifty *chroniques* [newspaper columns or feature articles] that were never collected into an edition during his life and that have been, by and large, overlooked by English translators. ³

In 1881 Maupassant's eminence was growing almost weekly and this had a great deal to do with his journalism and a series of articles criticizing patriotism, colonialism and war. ⁴ In an attempt to capitalize on Maupassant's name and boost the circulation of his paper, Meyer decided to unbridle Maupassant and send him as a special envoy to an Algeria seemingly on the precipice of a general Arab insurrection. The name of the rebel leader, Bou-Amama, was on everyone's lips in Paris, but information about this man, as Maupassant would find out (cf. *To the Sun*, ch. V), was thin on the ground and contradictory. Now, as then, there is a scarcity of material available on Bou-Amama and his uprising (particularly in English) ⁵ and Maupassant's writings on the rebellion and its causes form an important historical document.

Cheikh Mohammed ben Arbi-Hadji Bou-Amama (1833-1908) hailed from the western or *Ghâraba* branch of the tribal brotherhood of the Ouled Sidi Cheikh who had rebelled from 1864-70 and had maintained resistance to the advances and increased influences of French colonialism ever since. Bou-Amama founded a *Zaouïa* (a religious establishment) in Moghrar on the south-western border with Morocco in 1878 where he acquired a saintly reputation as a pious religious leader who lived an ascetic life. At this time the south-west of Algeria was largely untouched by Europeans and the one major military post, that of Géryville (now called El Bayadh), only really had a degree of control over a radius of 70-80 km. Miracles and divine favours were attributed to Bou-Amama by his followers and his influence and numbers of supporters grew, largely unimpaired by French authorities. It is unclear to what extent Bou-Amama initiated plans for insurrection or whether he was solicited by those around him to become the head of a movement, but he began to send out emissaries to sound out support from the tribes of the Sud-Oranais. Belatedly, the French powers reacted to this stoking up of the flames of insurrection and sent out Lieutenant Weinbrenner, the second in command of the *bureau arabe* of Géryville, to arrest two of Bou-Amama's envoys. Weinbrenner was murdered on April 21, 1881 and Bou-Amama was forced to declare a holy war earlier than he had intended. By the time of Maupassant's arrival in Algeria,

Introduction

Bou-Amama and his men had made raids on several towns in the south, been involved in a skirmish with French forces at Chellala, and had massacred nearly two hundred Spanish emigrants who worked on the esparto farms of the hauts plateaux, south of Saïda. Bou-Amama had made a mockery of the French army who, although vastly superior in arms and numbers, not only could not capture him, but barely even knew his whereabouts.

The fear of a general Muslim uprising in Algeria was understandable, but it never really materialized and Colonel Négrier[6] drove Bou-Amama into exile in Morocco in 1883. He established a new *Zaouïa* in Deldoul and incursions into southern Algeria began to increase in frequency from 1890-6, but in 1901 Bou-Amama offered his submission. Bou-Amama is still seen today as an important figure in the Algerian movement towards independence, but his resistance was on a relatively small scale and is glossed over in just two sentences in Charles-Robert Ageron's *Modern Algeria: A History from 1830 to the Present*.[7]

Maupassant travelled in Algeria for two months, returning to Paris in October following a stay on the island of Corsica.[8] During this time he sent back several *chroniques* and other articles in the form of letters which depicted a less praiseworthy mindlessness than that spoken of in his letter to Gisèlle d'Estoc, viz. the administration of Algeria and the absurdities of French colonialism. Gérard Delaisement points out that Maupassant divided his pieces into three categories, signing those of a descriptive nature and of general interest 'Guy de Maupassant'; those on military subjects 'un officier' [an officer]; and those on economic and administrative themes 'un colon' [a colonist].[9] The texts he submitted to *Le Gaulois* and their dates of publication were as follows:

'Alger à vol d'oiseau' (July 17, 1881).
'Lettres d'Afrique'—signed: un colon (July 20, 1881).
'Autour d'Oran' (July 26, 1881).
[Untitled letter, following after 'Autour d'Oran']—signed: un colon (July 26, 1881).
'Le Prisonnier' (July 28, 1881).
'Lettre d'Afrique'—signed: un officier (July 28, 1881).
'Sur les Hauts Plateaux' (July 31, 1881).
'Lettre d'Afrique'—signed: un colon (August 2, 1881).

'Les Oulad Naïl' (August 11, 1881).
'Lettre d'Afrique' (August 20, 1881).
'Le Ramadan' (August 25, 1881).
'Les Incendies en Algérie'—signed: *** (August 29, 1881).
'La Vie Arabe' (August 31, 1881).
'Le Feu en Kabylie'—signed: un colon (September 3, 1881).
'Lettre d'Afrique'—signed: un colon (September 7, 1881).
'Les Grands Chefs indigènes en Algérie'—signed: un colon (September 14, 1881).
'Dans le Désert. Paysages d'Afriques' (September 20, 1881).
'Les Oasis et le Mzab' (September 27, 1881).
'Le Pays du sel' (October 19, 1881).

The above articles were the source material from which *To the Sun* [*Au soleil*] was extracted. As Delaisement puts it, *To the Sun* was not a work written in 1884, but '*un «arrangement» de textes amendés, adoucis, corrigés*' ['an "arrangement" of amended, corrected and toned down texts'].[10] In addition to these pieces written for *Le Gaulois* as a direct result of his time in Algeria, Maupassant also utilized several later *chroniques* and a short story in compiling *To the Sun*, extracting some sentences verbatim, elsewhere rewriting them, or borrowing themes.[11] The new 'arrangement' was then published in the *Revue bleue*, serialized over the issues of November 17, 1883, December 1, 1883, December 15, 1883, and January 5, 1884. *To the Sun* was then issued in book form (Paris: Victor Havard, 1884) later in January, with a few minor changes to the text, mainly in spellings, and adjustments to the chapter titles and structure.

Also included in the first edition of the book were the *Fragments*, 'At the Spas' ['Aux Eaux'], 'In Brittany' ['En Bretagne'] and 'Le Creusot' ['Le Creusot']. The literary provenance of the *Fragments* was similar to that of *To the Sun*:

'At the Spas' was first published in *Le Gaulois* (July 24, 1883).

'In Brittany' featured in *Nouvelle Revue* (January 1, 1884) and was itself a reworking of several articles: 'Le Pays des Korrigans' (December 10, 1880), 'En Bretagne' (July 16, 1882), 'En Carême' (February 21, 1883)—all published in *Le Gaulois*—and 'Coins du Pays. La Pointe du Raz' (August 2, 1882), published in *Gil Blas*.

Introduction

'Le Creusot' first appeared as 'Petits Voyages. Le Creusot' (August 28, 1883) in *Gil Blas*.

It has been suggested, both justifiably and unfairly, that the *Fragments* were added simply to flesh out the book volume of *To the Sun*. The justification, as we have just witnessed above, is that Maupassant was no stranger to recycling material, knowing full well as an *industriel des lettres* how to eke out the maximum possible financial gain from his writing—setting out ideas first in his journalism, before collecting and reworking them for serialization in reviews and periodicals, then publishing them in book form, and sometimes even going on to license extracts from the books to be printed.[12] The suggestion is perhaps a little unfair in that the three *Fragments* complement *To the Sun* in their themes and imagery, highlighting the idea that travel, adventure, and 'the other' can be found next door as well as in distant lands. The wilderness of Brittany's moors and coastlines (in 'In Brittany') and the immensity of the Alpine mountains and ravines (in 'At the Spas') can leave the reader feeling as diminutive and awestruck as the boundless, arid plains and deserts of Algeria. Meanwhile in the volume closer 'Le Creusot', which on the surface may appear to have little in connection to Maupassant's account of Algeria, we are given a description of a smelting works where the power and strength of the heat and fire remind us of the majesty and power of the sun in *To the Sun*, and the description of such an industrial process draws a contrast with the simplistic, nomadic life led in the desert.

Maupassant's trip to Algeria in 1881 had a profound impact on him and he would return to the country a further three times in later life.[13] His travels and experiences in North Africa would furnish his short fiction with settings and scenarios,[14] and would provide a background to one of Maupassant's most famous characters, Georges Duroy, the hero of *Bel-Ami* (Paris: Victor Havard, 1885), who, like Maupassant, is a journalist who first makes his name with a series of articles on his experiences (as an officer) in Algeria. Since the time of first publication, readers and critics have speculated as to the autobiographical content of Maupassant's novels, and Maupassant would play up to suggestions that Georges Duroy was based upon himself by signing copies of the novel 'Bel Ami'.[15] But of Maupassant's published works, it is in his travel writing, not his fiction, that he is most candid with his inner thoughts and feelings: the deep sense of despair and alienation that plagued him, and his constant need to escape. Maupassant's pessimism is perhaps most clearly expressed in his second travel book, *Sur l'eau* [*Afloat*] (Paris: Marpon et Flammarion, 1888), with such sentiments as

> Can it be true that no one has yet felt hatred of the human face which is always the same, hatred of animals which seem like living mechanisms with their unvarying instincts transmitted in their seed from the first of their race to the last, hatred of landscapes eternally the same, and hatred of pleasures never renewed?[16]

And

> It is true that, on certain days, I feel horror of what exists, to the point of wishing to be dead. I sense to the point of acute pain the unchanging monotony of the landscape, of faces and of thoughts. The mediocrity of the universe astonishes and repels me, the pettiness of everything fills me with disgust, the inadequacy of human beings overwhelms me.[17]

But such thoughts were already present in *To the Sun*, the opening chapter perfectly summing up the ennui and escapist desires that would hound Maupassant throughout his life. And whereas *To the Sun* is a more descriptive, political, and analytical piece of travel writing in comparison to the more introspective *Sur l'eau*, there is nevertheless present in its language a reflection of Maupassant's quest to lose himself. He is always looking to the far away horizon, as he stands in landscapes described as *boundless*, *limitless*, or *interminable*. In such expanses man and all his achievements are dwarfed and Maupassant's prose constantly brings us back to the light and the *ferocious* or *crushing* heat of the sun, to whom the book is an ode, and whose immense powers over the lands he is travelling through make all attempts at ownership seem futile.

In *To the Sun* we have an account of a land and populace vanquished by the twin powers of the sun and French colonialism. Maupassant bows down before the former, finding a personal absolution in the light, heat, and space of the desert. He stands up to the latter, however, pointing out the faults, limitations and absurdities of French colonialism, all the while demonstrating his brilliance as a political reporter who came to understand Algeria and its problems in such a

Introduction

short space of time. As we continue to bear witness to the fallout from colonialism in Africa and the Middle East and the frictions between Western and Islamic culture, To the Sun remains as relevant today as when it was written.

Notes

[1] Guy de Maupassant, Letter to Gisèle d'Estoc from Algiers [all translations are mine unless stated otherwise], in Correspondance, ed. Jacques Suffel, 3 vols. (Évreux: Cercle du Bibliophile, 1973), vol. II, no. 239, p. 41. D'Estoc (1863-1907) was one of Maupassant's mistresses.

[2] Paul Ignotus, The Paradox of Maupassant (London: University of London Press, 1966), p. 155.

[3] The best edition in French is Chroniques de Maupassant, ed. Gérard Delaisement, 2 vols. (Paris: Rive Droite, 2003).

[4] Maupassant's articles 'La Guerre' (April 10, 1881), 'Le Respect' (April 22, 1881), 'Balançoires' (May 12, 1881), and 'Zut' (July 5, 1881), all published in Le Gaulois, expressed his condemnation and horror of the monstrous absurdity of war at a time when France was moving troops into Tunisia (in which Italy also had an interest), eventually making it a French protectorate. For a translation of 'La Guerre', see Guy de Maupassant, Afloat [Sur l'eau, 1888], tr. Marlo Johnston (London: Peter Owen, 1995), pp. 117-23.

[5] In French, accounts of the rebellion include: Colonel Innocenti, Insurrection du Sud-Oranais en 1881: Bou-Amema et le Colonel Innocenti (Paris: Téqui, 1893); Capitaine Armengaud, Le Sud Oranais: Journal d'un Légionnaire (Paris and Limoges: Henri Charles-Lavauzelle, 1893); and Commandant E Graulle, Insurrection de Bou-Amama (Avril 1881) (Paris: Henri Charles-Lavauzelle, 1905).

[6] François-Oscar de Négrier (1839-1913), French general.

[7] Charles-Robert Ageron, Modern Algeria: A History from 1830 to the Present, tr. Michael Brett (Trenton, NJ: Africa World Press, Inc., 1991), p. 53.

[8] For the dating of Maupassant's return, cf. his letter to Gisèle d'Estoc from Bou-Saada, August 25, 1881, in Correspondance, vol. II, no. 243, p. 52, in which he says he will leave Algeria from Bône (now called Annaba) on September 10, intends to stay in

Bastia on Corsica until October 1, and hopes to return to Paris towards October 15.

[9] Gérard Delaisement, 'Les chroniques coloniales de Maupassant', in *Maupassant et l'écriture: Actes du colloque de Fécamp 21-22-23 Mai 1993*, ed. Louis Forestier (Paris: Editions Nathan, 1993), p. 54.

[10] Ibid., p. 53.

[11] The later *chroniques* are: 'La Pitié' (December 22, 1881); 'Chronique' (June 14, 1882); and 'Le Haut et le Bas' (March 16, 1883), all of which appeared in *Le Gaulois*. The short story is 'La Peur', which first appeared in *Le Gaulois* (October 23, 1882) and was later included in the collection *Contes de la bécasse* (Paris: Rouveyre et Blond, 1883). Maupassant also reworked his description of Marseille in 'La Patrie de Columba' published in *Le Gaulois* (September 27, 1880) for the opening of the second chapter of *To the Sun*, 'The Sea'. For an analysis of Maupassant's source material for *To the Sun*, and how he reused it, see Gérard Delaisement, 'La Composition des «Carnets de Voyages» de Guy de Maupassant: *Au Soleil, Sur l'eau, La Vie errante* (avec des documents inédits)', in *Revue des Sciences Humaines*, Oct-Dec 1958, pp. 531-54; and Guy de Maupassant, *Carnets de Voyage*, ed. Gérard Delaisement (Paris: Rive Droite, 2006).

[12] Delaisement points out in 'La Composition des «Carnets de Voyages» de Guy de Maupassant', p. 552, that Maupassant published a chapter of *To the Sun* going under the guise of a different title, 'La Vie au désert', in *Le Voleur* (March 20, 1884).

[13] Maupassant's second trip to Algeria and Tunisia was from October 4, 1887-January 6, 1888, and is recounted in chapters V-VII of his third travel book *La Vie errante* [The Wandering Life] (Paris: Ollendorff, 1890); his third trip was from October 20, 1888 until the following spring, 1889; his fourth trip lasted some three months from September 6, 1890. Unlike his first journey, the later ones were made not as a journalist, but for pleasure and health reasons. For the dating of these voyages see Denise Brahimi 'Présentation', in Guy de Maupassant, *Écrits sur Le Maghreb*, ed. Denise Brahimi (Paris: Minerve, 1988), p. 6; and Michael G Lerner, *Maupassant* (London: George Allen & Unwin Ltd, 1975), p. 249.

[14] Stories notably influenced by Maupassant's African sojourns include 'La Peur' (see n. 11); 'Marroca', first published in *Gil Blas*, March 2, 1882 and then included in *Mademoiselle Fifi* (Bruxelles: Kistemaekers, 1882); 'L'Orient', first published in *Le Gaulois*, September 13, 1883 (this piece is sometimes considered a *chronique* rather than a *conte*); 'Mohammed-Fripouille', first published in *Le Gaulois*, September 20, 1884 and then included in *Yvette* (Paris: Victor Havard, 1885); 'Un soir', first published

in *L'Illustration*, January 19 and 26, 1889 and then included in *La Main gauche* (Paris: Ollendorff, 1889); and 'Allouma', first published in *L'Écho de Paris*, February 10 and 15, 1889 and then included in *La Main gauche*.

[15] Michael G Lerner, *Maupassant*, p. 204. Alongside *Bel-Ami*, Maupassant's *Notre coeur* (Paris: Ollendorff, 1890) is also considered a *roman-à-clef*.

[16] Guy de Maupassant, *Afloat*, tr. Marlo Johnston, p. 40.

[17] Ibid., p. 51.

Select Bibliography

Editions of *To the Sun*

French

Au Soleil (Paris: Victor Havard, 1884), 297 pp. First edition.

Au Soleil, vol. XXVI (1904), ill. André Suréda / engraved by G Lemoine, of *Oeuvres complètes illustrées*, 30 vols. (Paris: Société d'éditions litteraires et artistiques, Librairie Paul Ollendorff, 1901-4, 1912), 305 pp.

Au Soleil, vol. VIII (1908) of *Oeuvres complètes de Guy de Maupassant*, ed. Pol Neveux, 29 vols. (Paris: Louis Conard, 1908-10), 295 pp. AS followed by the Corsican *chroniques* 'La Patrie de Colomba', 'Le Monastère de Corbara', 'Les Bandits Corses' and 'Une page d'histoire inédite'.

Au Soleil, vol. IX (1935), ill. Vergé-Sarrat, w. 'Notice' by René Dumesnil, of *Oeuvres complètes illustrées de Guy de Maupassant*, ed. René Dumesnil and Jean Loize, 15 vols. (Paris: Librairie de France, 1934-8), 365 pp. In this volume AS is followed by the Corsican *chroniques* 'La Patrie de Colomba', 'Le Monastère de Corbara', 'Les Bandits Corses' and 'Une page d'histoire inédite'. Then comes *La Vie errante*, which is followed by the *chroniques* 'Venise', 'Ischia', and 'Pêcheuses et Guerrières', then two of the *Fragments*, 'Le Creusot' and 'En Bretagne', ending with 'Le voyage du «Horla»'.

Au Soleil, vol. XIV, ill. André Suréda / engraved by G Lemoine, of *Oeuvres complètes*, ed. Gilbert Sigaux, 16 vols. (Lausanne: Editions Rencontre, 1961-2), 397 pp. AS with *Sur l'eau*.

Au Soleil, vol. XIII (1970), ill. Francine Simonin, of *Oeuvres complètes de Maupassant*, ed. Pascal Pia, 17 vols. (Paris: M Gonon and Evreux: Cercle du Bibliophile, 1969-73), 489 pp. AS with *Sur l'eau* and *La Vie errante*.

Maupassant au Maghreb: d'Alger à Tunis, Tunis, vers Kairouan, ed. Denise Brahimi (Paris: le Sycomore, 1982), 337 pp. A facsimile of the 1884 edition of AS minus the *Fragments* and the 1890 edition of *La Vie errante* (chapters V-VII).

Écrits sur le Maghreb, ed. Denise Brahimi (Paris: Minerve, 1988), 190 pp. AS minus the three *Fragments*, coupled with chapters V-VII of *La Vie errante*.

Au Soleil, ill. Jean-Baptiste Valadié, in *Romans et récits de voyage*, vol. III of *Oeuvres*, 4 vols. (Club de l'honnête homme, 1987), 482 pp.

Écrits sur le Maghreb: récits, nouvelles, lettres, ed. Denise Brahimi (Paris: Minerve, 1991), 249 pp. A revised and expanded version of the 1988 edition above, including some of Maupassant's correspondence from his journeys to North Africa and the short stories 'Marroca', 'Mohammed-Fripouille' and 'Allouma'.

'En Bretagne', vol. 2 of a boxed five-volume set of *Pour Gustave Flaubert; En Bretagne; De Tunis à Kairouan; Sur l'eau*; and *En Sicile* (Bruxelles: Éditions Complexe, 1993), 38 pp.

Lettres d'Afrique (Algérie, Tunisie), ed. Michèle Salinas (Paris: La Boîte à Documents, 1997), 366 pp. Contains the *Revue bleue* version of AS (that is, without the *Fragments*); five *chroniques* from 1881 relating to colonialism and war: 'L'«Affaire Tunisienne»', 'Balançoires', 'Vive Mustapha!', 'Zut!', and 'Choses du jour'; the July-October 1881 Algerian *chroniques* (see my Introduction for the list); and later African-themed *chroniques* (from December 1888-April 1891): 'Afrique', 'Mosquée & Zaouïa', 'Tunis', 'Promenade à travers Tunis', 'Vers Kairouan', 'Les Africaines', and 'Une fête arabe'.

Au Soleil et autres récits de voyages, ed. Gérard Gengembre (Paris: Pocket, 1998), 230 pp. Alongside full critical apparatus, also contains chapters I-III of *La Vie errante* and two *chroniques*, 'Venise' and 'Ischia'.

Au Soleil, ed. Alain Deshaies, ill. André Suréda (Paris: Nouvelle librairie de France, 1999), 225 pp.

Guy de Maupassant sur les chemins d'Algérie, ed. Jean Emmanuel, with a preface by Olivier Frébourg (Paris: Magellan & Cie, 2003), 189 pp. A collection of Maupassant's writings on Algeria including his letters and short stories, with 50 illustrations and photos of the period.

Récits d'Afrique, ed. Noëlle Benhamou (Lyon: Éditions Palimpseste, 2005), 253 pp. Contains AS with chapters V-VII of *La Vie errante* and critical apparatus.

Carnets de Voyage, ed. Gérard Delaisement (Paris: Rive Droite, 2006), 558 pp. Maupassant's three travel books, with a lengthy study and notes by Delaisement. AS is coupled with the Corsican *chroniques* 'La Patrie de Colomba', 'Le Monastère de Corbara', and 'Bandits Corses', and two of the *Fragments*, 'En Bretagne' and 'Le Creusot'. *Sur l'eau* is joined by the *chronique* 'Livre de Bord'; *La Vie errante* is joined by 'Venise' and 'Ischia'.

Au Soleil (Paris: Rive Droite, 2006), 225 pp. Large print edition.

English

Au Soleil or African Wanderings, tr. © Walter Dunne, vol. XII of *The Life Work of Henri René Guy de Maupassant*, 17 vols. (London and New York: Walter Dunne, 1903), 154 and 163 pp. This volume 'printed for subscribers only by The St Dunston Society', is illustrated and sees AS coupled with *La Vie Errante or In Vagabondia*. The translation is fairly loose and dated, toning down or omitting entirely certain passages, whilst paying little attention to Maupassant's style. This edition of Maupassant's works has been further discredited by Francis Steegmuller's revelation that it included some sixty-five short stories that weren't even by Maupassant! (See Francis Steegmuller, *Maupassant* (London: Collins, 1950), pp. 319-26.)

To the Sun, tr. James Wilson, in *The Use of English*, vol. 58, No. 3, Summer 2007, pp. 228-43. The first four chapters of AS.

Biographies and Studies of Maupassant in English

Ball, Bertrand Logan, *Love and Nature, Unity and Doubling in the Novels of Maupassant*, ed. Helen Roulston, American University Studies, Series II: Romance Languages and Literature, vol. 79 (New York: Peter Lang, 1988), 152 pp.

Boyd, Ernest, *Guy de Maupassant: A Biographical Study* (London and New York: Alfred A Knopf, 1926), 258 pp.

Bryant, David, *The Rhetoric of Pessimism and Strategies of Containment in the Short Stories of Guy de Maupassant*, vol. 7 of Studies in French Literature (Lewinston, NY, Lampeter, Wales, and Queenston, Canada: The Edwin Mellen Press, 1993), 190 pp.

Coulter, Stephen, *Damned shall be Desire: The Passionate Life of Guy de Maupassant* (London: Jonathan Cape, 1958), 350 pp. A novelization of Maupassant's life.

Donaldson-Evans, Mary, *A Woman's Revenge: The Chronology of Dispossession in Maupassant's fiction* (Lexington, KY: French Forum, Publishers, 1986), 159 pp.

Dugan, John Raymond, *Illusion and Reality: A Study of Descriptive Techniques in the Works of Guy de Maupassant* (The Hague and Paris: Mouton, 1973), 209 pp.

Fusco, Richard, *Maupassant and the American Short Story: The Influence of Form at the Turn of the Century* (University Park, PA: Pennsylvania State University Press, 1994), 230 pp.

Harris, Trevor A Le V, *Maupassant in the Hall of Mirrors: Ironies of Repetition in the Work of Guy de Maupassant* (Basingstoke: Macmillan, 1990), 230 pp.

Hartig, Rachel Mildred, *Struggling under the Destructive Glance: Androgyny in the Novels of Guy de Maupassant* (New York: P Lang, 1991), 134 pp.

Ignotus, Paul, *The Paradox of Maupassant* (London: University of London Press Ltd, 1966), 288 pp.

Jackson, Stanley, *Guy de Maupassant* (London: Duckworth, 1938), 310 pp.

Kirkbride, Ronald de Levington, *The Private Life of Guy de Maupassant* (New York: Sears Publishing Co., 1932), 252 pp.

Lerner, Michael G, *Maupassant* (London: George Allen & Unwin Ltd, 1975), 301 pp.

Macnamara, Matthew, *Style and vision in Maupassant's Nouvelles* (Berne and New York: P Lang, 1986), 247 pp.

Poteau-Tralie, Mary L, *Voices of Authority. Criminal Obsession in Guy de Maupassant's Short Works* (New York: Peter Lang, 1994), 146 pp.

Sherard, Robert Harborough, *The Life, Work and Evil Fate of Guy de Maupassant (Gentilhomme de lettres)* (London: T Werner Laurie LTD., 1926), 399 pp.

Steegmuller, Francis, *Maupassant* (London: Collins, 1950), 384 pp; repr. as *Maupassant: A Lion in the Path* (London: Macmillan, 1972), 430 pp.

Stivale, Charles J, *The Art of Rupture: Narrative Desire and Duplicity in the Tales of Guy de Maupassant* (Ann Arbor, MI: The University of Michigan Press, 1994, repr. 1997), 264 pp.

Sullivan, Edward D, *Maupassant: The Novelist* (Princeton, NJ: Princeton University Press, 1954), 199 pp.

Sullivan, Edward D, *Maupassant: The Short Stories* (London: Edward Arnold (Publishers) LTD., 1962), 64 pp.

Wallace, A H, *Guy de Maupassant*, Twayne's World Authors Series, no. 265 (New York: Twayne Publishers, Inc., 1973), 156 pp.

Studies and Articles with relevance to *To the Sun*

(See also the introductions to the editions of Benhamou, Brahimi, Delaisement, Gengembre, and Salinas listed above.)

Alderer, Adolphe, 'Au soleil', in *Le Temps*, January 31, 1884.

Bendahan, Blanche, 'Un Grand Normand en Algérie', in *Algérie*, July-August, 1950.

Bienvenu, Jacques (ed.), *Maupassant et les pays du soleil: actes du colloque de Marseille, 1er et 2 juin 1997* (Paris: Klincksieck, 1999), 147 pp.

Dagron, Chantal, 'Déserts sublimes. Variations et contrepoints', in *Revue des Sciences Humaines*, 'Le Désert, l'espace et l'esprit', no. 258, May-June 2000, pp. 267-88.

Delaisement, Gérard, 'La Composition des «Carnets de Voyages» de Guy de Maupassant: *Au Soleil, Sur l'eau, La Vie errante* (avec des documents inédits)', in *Revue des Sciences Humaines*, Oct-Dec 1958.

Delaisement, Gérard, 'Les chroniques coloniales de Maupassant', in *Maupassant et l'écriture: Actes du colloque de Fécamp 21-22-23 Mai 1993*, ed. Louis Forestier (Paris: Editions Nathan, 1993).

Dugan, John Raymond, ch. IV 'The Travel Books', in *Illusion and Reality: A Study of Descriptive Techniques in the Works of Guy de Maupassant* (The Hague and Paris: Mouton, 1973), pp. 59-69.

Dupuy, Aimé, 'L'Algérie dans l'oeuvre de Maupassant', in *Documents algériens*, Série culturelle, no. 51, December 26, 1950.

Gouaux-Coutrix, Mireille, 'Au Soleil ou un romancier face à la colonisation', in Minorités, échanges, populations et l'individu: actes du colloque international Entre l'Occident et l'Orient: Antibes-Juan les Pins, 29-31 octobre 1981, organized by the Université de Nice, Laboratoire d'histoire quantative (Nice: Université de Nice, 1983).

Hourant, Georges-Pierre, 'Maupassant et l'Algérie', in L'Algerianiste, no. 47, September 1989.

Magri-Mourgues, Véronique, 'Du récit de voyage à la nouvelle. L'exemple de Maupassant: Au Soleil, Marroca, Mohammed-Fripouille, Un Soir, Allouma', in Roman et récit de voyage, ed. Philippe Antoine et Marie-Christine Gomez-Géraud (Paris: Presses de l'Université de Paris Sorbonne, 2001), pp.155-66.

Mélia, Jean, 'Guy de Maupassant Algérien', in the Supplement littéraire of Figaro, September 5, 1925.

Mélia, Jean, 'Le premier voyage de Maupassant en Algérie', in Algeria, no. 50, April, 1930.

Mélia, Jean, 'Le deuxième voyage', in Documents algériens, Série culturelle, no. 51, December 26, 1950.

Meter, Helmut, 'Expériences du désert dans le récit de voyage au XIXe siècle. Fromentin, Maupassant, Loti', in Le génie du lieu: expériences du ravissement, du transport, de la dépossession, ed. Helmut Meter et Pierre Glaudes (Münster and London: Lit. Cop., 2003), pp.45-61.

Schapira, Marie-Claude, 'Guy de Maupassant en Algérie: critique du fait colonial et portrait du colonisé', in L'idée de "race" dans les sciences humaines et la littérature, XVIIIe-XIXe siècles: actes du colloque international de Lyon, 16-18 novembre 2000, ed. Sarga Moussa (Paris, Budapest and Torino: L'Harmattan, 2003), pp. 329-41.

Soubias, Pierre, 'La place de l'Afrique dans l'imaginaire de Maupassant: Une lecture des nouvelles africaines', in Maupassant multiple: actes du colloque de Toulouse, 13-15 décembre 1993, ed. Yves Reboul (Toulouse: Presses universitaires du Mirail, 1995), pp. 29-39.

Stefanson, Blandine, 'Maupassant et le colonialisme', in Essays in French literature, no. 30, November 1993, pp. 30-62.

Tassart, François, 'Maupassant en Algérie', ed. Pierre Cogny, in Les Oeuvres libres, vol. 188, January 1962 (Paris: Librairie Fayard, 1961), pp. 97-134.

Select Bibliography

Zouaghi Keime, Marie-Anne, 'Genèse d'une passion: Maupassant et l'appel du Sud', in *Actes du quatrième colloque international et pluridisciplinaire sur l'écriture du voyage, 2-4 juillet 2003* (Ankara: üniversitesi Basimevi, 2004), pp. 249-56.

Chronology of Maupassant's Life and Works

1850—August 5, Henry René Albert Guy de Maupassant born at the Château de Miromesnil in Tourville-sur-Arques, near Dieppe, the son of Gustave (1821-99), a notary, and Laure de Maupassant (née Le Poittevin, 1821-1904), a childhood friend of Flaubert (1821-80) and Louis Bouilhet (1822-69).
1854—The Maupassants move to the Château d'Ymauville, in Grainville-Ymauville, near Le Havre.
1856—Birth of Guy's younger brother, Hervé de Maupassant.
1858—The Maupassants spend the summer at the coastal fishing village and resort of Etretat where they buy a house, *Les Verguies*, Laure and Hervé moving there the following year.
1859—Gustave employed at a Paris bank, the family move to Passy.
1859-60—Guy at school at the Lycée Napoléon, Paris.
1860-2—Marriage between Gustave and Laure breaks up, Gustave remains in Paris, Laure moves with the two boys to Etretat.
1863—Guy enrolled at a Catholic boarding school, the Institution Ecclésiastique in Yvetot. Legal separation of Gustave and Laure.
1867—Guy expelled for writing 'obscene' verses. He becomes a boarder at the Lycée Corneille in Rouen, where Bouilhet, a poet and the city librarian, acts as his guardian and encourages his writing.
1868—At Etretat Guy meets Algernon Charles Swinburne (1837-1909), having been in one of the fishing boats that went to the poet's rescue as he was drowning.

1869—Guy receives his *baccalauréat*. Bouilhet introduces Guy to Flaubert. Death of Bouilhet. Guy enrols at law school in Paris.

1870—July 15, France declares war on Prussia, Guy enlists voluntarily. September 1, French defeated at Sedan.

1871—January 28, French surrender, end of Siege of Paris (from September 19, 1870). Paris Commune until May 28. Maupassant discharged from the army in November.

1872—Guy becomes an unsalaried civil servant at the Ministry of the Marine and Colonies, in Paris; he is living in a ground floor flat at 2 rue Moncey, Montmartre. Spends his free time boating along the Seine at Argenteuil, Chatou, Bougival and Sartrouville, a passion that had been engendered in his childhood and would last all his life.

1873—Guy graduates to a paid position at the Ministry. He begins to see more and more of Flaubert, who oversees his literary pursuits.

1875—Publication, under the pseudonym of Joseph Prunier, of his story 'La Main d'écorché' in the provincial paper *Almanach lorrain de Pont-à-Mousson*— Maupassant's first published work. First private performance of his play *À la feuille de rose, maison turque*. Maupassant writes his one-act comedy *Une Répétition* (publ. Paris: Tresse, 1879, in *Saynètes et monologues*, 6th series).

1876—Increasingly a part of the Parisian literary scene, having published some poems, articles and stories under various pseudonyms. Through Flaubert he began to mix in literary circles, including such figures as Émile Zola (1840-1902), Edmond de Goncourt (1822-96), Alphonse Daudet (1840-97), Henry James, jr. (1843-1916), Catulle Mendès (1841-1909), Stéphane Mallarmé (1842-98), Auguste compte de Villiers de L'Isle-Adam (1838-89), and Ivan Turgenev (1818-83). Maupassant becomes a part of the Médan group of writers gathered around Zola, also consisting of Paul Alexis (1847-1901), Joris-Karl Huysmans (1848-1907), Léon Hennique (1851-1935), and Henry Céard (1851-1924). Maupassant starts to write his drama in verse, *La Trahison de la Comtesse de Rhune*. Moves to 17 rue Clauzel, Montmartre.

1877—Second performance of *À la feuille de rose, maison turque*. In August receives leave to visit Switzerland on health grounds, Maupassant aware of his having contracted syphilis. In December begins to plan a novel *Une Vie*.

Chronology

1878—Maupassant transfers to the Ministry of Education.

1879—February 19, Maupassant's play *Histoire du vieux temps* performed in Paris (publ. Paris: Tresse, 1879). September, travels in Brittany.

1880—January, Maupassant ordered to appear before a magistrate for an 'outrage against decency and public morality' regarding the publication of his poem 'Une Fille', in the *Revue moderne et naturaliste*, November 1, 1879. A letter of defence from Flaubert, printed in *Le Gaulois*, February 21, combined with the fact that the poem, with the different title of 'Au bord de l'eau', had already appeared three years earlier without stir in Catulle Mendès' magazine *République des Lettres*, March 20, 1876, meant that the prosecution was dropped by February 27. April, 'Boule de suif' published in *Les Soirées de Médan* (Paris: Charpentier). Also publishes a volume of poetry, *Des Vers* (Paris: Charpentier) and begins to write for *Le Gaulois*. May 8, Death of Flaubert. September-October, travels to Corsica. In Paris moves to larger apartment at 83 rue Dulong. Probably around this time that he begins his relationship with Gisèle d'Estoc (pseud. Marie-Paule Desbarres, 1863-1907).

1881—May, publication of *La Maison Tellier* (Paris: Victor Havard), a collection of short stories. July-September, travels in Algeria as correspondent for *Le Gaulois*.

1882—Short story collection *Mademoiselle Fifi* (Bruxelles: Kistemaekers). After a series of periods of extended leave, officially leaves his post at the Ministry of Education to make his living from his writing. Travels in Brittany in the summer.

1883—First novel *Une Vie* published (Paris: Victor Havard). Short story collections *Contes de la bécasse* (Paris: Rouveyre et Blond), *Mademoiselle Fifi, nouveaux contes* (enlarged edition, Paris: Victor Havard). Buys a house which he names *La Guillette* in Etretat. Employs his valet, François Tassart, who stays in his service for the rest of Maupassant's life. July, at the watering place of Châtel-Guyon in the Auvergne.

1884—January, *To the Sun* [*Au Soleil*] published (Paris: Victor Havard); rents an apartment in Cannes and will henceforth largely divide his time between there, le cap d'Antibes, Etretat and Paris. In Paris moves to 10 rue Montchanin, taking the ground floor of his cousin Louis Le Poittevin's

(1847-1909) house. Short story collections *Clair de Lune* (Paris: E Monnier), *Miss Harriet* (Paris: Victor Havard), *Les Soeurs Rondoli* (Paris: Ollendorff). In this year Maupassant forges many of his more intimate and long-lasting relationships with women. In the spring he spends time in Etretat with Clémence Brun-Chabas, Hermine Lecomte du Noüy (1855-1915), and Blanche Roosevelt Macchetta Tucker (1853-98). Maupassant is a regular of many society salons, being one of the male 'Macchabées' (so-called because they were apparently willing to die for their hostess) gathered around Countess Emmanuela Potocka (née Pignatelli, 1852-1943); he also visits the houses of the Warshawski (or Warchawsky) sisters, Loulia Cahen d'anvers (1854-1918) and Marie Kann (1861-1928)—both of whom may have been his lovers. Maupassant is also introduced to the future Mme Straus (née Geneviève Halévy, 1849-1926).

*1885—Second novel *Bel-Ami* (Paris: Victor Havard). Short story collections *Yvette* (Paris: Victor Havard), *Contes du Jour et de la Nuit* (Paris: Marpon et Flammarion), *Contes et nouvelles* (Paris: Charpentier). Travels in Italy (April-May). August, takes waters at Châtel-Guyon.

1886—Short story collections *Toine* (Paris: Marpon et Flammarion), *Monsieur Parent* (Paris: Ollendorff), *La Petite Roque* (Paris: Victor Havard), *Contes choisis* (Paris: Librairie illustrée). Travels to England in the spring. January, rents villa in Antibes, from where he goes sailing on his newly purchased yacht the *Bel-Ami* later in the year with his faithful crew of valet François, skipper Raymond and mate Bernard. July, at Châtel-Guyon. In summer rents *Maison Fournais* in Chatou.

1887—Third novel *Mont-Oriol* (Paris: Victor Havard). Short story collection *Le Horla* (Paris: Ollendorff). March-April, yachting off Antibes in *Bel-Ami*. July 8, hot-air balloon voyage from La Villette to Heyst-sur-Mer in balloon named *Le Horla*. October, travels in Algeria and Tunisia (until January 1888).

1888—Fourth novel *Pierre et Jean* (Paris: Ollendorff). Second travel book *Sur l'eau* (Paris: Marpon et Flammarion). Short story collections *Le Rosier de Madame Husson* (Paris: Quantin), *L'Héritage* (Paris: Marpon et Flammarion). March-April, yachting off Cannes in *Bel-Ami*. Worsening health leads to stays at Aix-les-Bains in April and October. June, second balloon voyage in *Le Horla*. October, further travels to North Africa (until January 1889).

1889—Fifth novel *Fort comme la mort* (Paris: Ollendorff). Short story collection *La Main gauche* (Paris: Ollendorff). January, buys new yacht (again renamed *Bel-Ami*) and goes sailing off Italian coast in October. In summer rents villa in Triel-sur-Seine. November 3, death of Hervé de Maupassant, insane, in an asylum. In Paris moves to 14 avenue Victor Hugo.

1890—Third travel book *La Vie errante* (Paris: Ollendorff). Sixth novel *Notre coeur* (Paris: Ollendorff). Short story collections *L'Inutile Beauté* (Paris: Victor Havard), *Histoire d'une fille de ferme* (Paris: Marpon et Flammarion). In Paris moves to 24 rue Boccador. Begins *L'Angélus*, a novel that will remain unfinished at Maupassant's death. June-September, staying in Aix-les-Bains, and in Plombières-les-Bains and Gérardmer in the Vosges département. September-November, travels once more to Algeria.

1891—Play *Musotte*, written with Jacques Normand (1848-1931), performed successfully at Théâtre du Gymnase (publ. Paris: Ollendorff, 1891). June-August, staying in Divonne-les-Bains in the Jura mountains. September, at Aix-les-Bains. From November at the Chalet de l'Isère, in Cannes.

1892—Night of January 1/2, attempted suicide in Cannes. January 7 admitted, insane, into Dr Blanche's clinic, in Passy.

1893—March, comedy *La Paix de Ménage* staged at Théâtre Français (publ. Paris: Ollendorff, 1893). July 6, death of Maupassant. July 8, buried in Montparnasse.

1897—Posthumous collection of stories *Trois contes* (Paris: Gautier).

1899—Posthumous collection of stories *Le Père Milon* (Paris: Ollendorff).

1900—Posthumous collection of stories *Le Colporteur* (Paris: Ollendorff).

Note to the Text

The translation is based upon the text of the first edition, *Au Soleil* (Paris: Victor Havard, 1884), in consultation with *Au Soleil et autres récits de voyages*, ed. Gérard Gengembre (Paris: Pocket, 1998) and *Les Carnets de Voyage de Guy de Maupassant*, ed. Gérard Delaisement (Paris: Rive Droite, 2006). The translation follows the first edition in paragraph structure and emphasis (italics, small caps etc.). I have imported some words—mainly technical terms, relating to the military and colonial administration, or words of an Arabic or Islamic origin—from the French text into the English translation wholesale, putting them into italics and explaining them, where necessary, on their first occurrence in the endnotes. These words and phrases, in alphabetical order are as follows: *Algérien(s)*; *arbico*; *bureau(x) arabe(s)*; *caïd*; *chahuts*; *cïé mosieu*; *(commune) mixte*; *commune de plein exercice*; *connétable*; *de grande tente*; *douar(s)*; *gandoura*; *goum(s)*; *goumiers*; *gourbis*; *Joanne*; *kadis*; *korrigan(s)*; *koubba(s)*; *kouskoussou*; *ksar*; *léfaa(s)*; *méci mosieu*; *ouran*; *places militaires*; *roumis*; *Sebkra*; *turcos*; *vipère céraste*. Outside of these words and phrases, emphasis is Maupassant's. Editorial insertions and clarifications appear in square brackets. Maupassant sometimes gives capital letters to words of a geographical nature such as *Sud*, *Océan*, and *Désert*, but not always—his capitalization is followed in this translation. He is also inconsistent in his capitalization of titles, such as *agha* and *bach'agha*, again the first edition is followed here. The first edition spelling of place names has been kept throughout, except for those places where a common English alternative is in use (I think the only example is Algiers for *Alger*). Maupassant sometimes spells the same place name in different ways, this inconsistency is silently corrected, the most common spelling being chosen. A table of the Algerian place names used in *To the Sun* and their modern equivalents can be found in the Appendix.

In the wake of postcolonial theory and Orientalism, when dealing with texts on colonialism, one can encounter certain loaded words that take on a particular importance. For this reason, the French word *moeurs*, which may be translated variously as 'habits', 'customs', and 'morals' has been given in the text in square brackets after its translation, allowing the reader to agree or disagree with the translator's adjudgement of its relation to morality, behaviour or tradition.

Finally, a word on the choice of title. The rather literal rendering of *Au Soleil* as *To the Sun* was decided as it reflects both the geographical movement towards sunnier climes and the lyrical ode to the sun that the French title suggests.

To the Sun
[Au Soleil]

To Pol Arnault [1]

I

Life, so short, so long, at times becomes unbearable, always unfolding the same way with death at its end. You can't stop it, or change it, can't even understand it, and every so often, in the face of the sheer impotence of our efforts, an indignation rears up and seizes hold of us. No matter what we do, we will die! No matter what we believe, what we think, what we try, we will die. It seems we will die tomorrow still knowing nothing, nevertheless disgusted by all that we do know. And so you feel crushed by 'the eternal wretchedness of all things',[2] by man's helplessness and the monotony of his actions.

You get up, you walk, you lean on your elbow at the window. The people opposite are having lunch, just as they had lunch yesterday, and just as they'll have lunch tomorrow: the father, mother, and four children. Three years ago the grandmother was still there. But no longer. The father has changed a lot since we've been neighbours.[3] He doesn't notice it in himself, he seems content; he seems happy. Imbecile!

They talk about a marriage, then a death, then about their chicken which is tender, then their servant who isn't honest. They worry about a thousand useless and foolish things. Imbeciles!

The sight of their apartment, in which they have lived for eighteen years, fills me with disgust and indignation. And that's what it is, that's life! Four walls, two doors, a window, a bed, some chairs, a table, there you go! It's a prison, a prison! Anywhere you live for a long time becomes a prison! Oh! to flee, to leave! to flee the familiar places, the people, the same routines, and above all the same thoughts!

When you are tired, tired of moping about from morning till night, tired of not having the energy to even get up and drink a glass of water, tired of the faces of friends seen too often and now irritating, tired of odious and placid neighbours, of familiar and monotonous things, of your house, of your road, of your servant who has just said, 'What would Sir like for dinner?' and who leaves, emphasizing each pace, the frayed hem of her dirty skirt scraping along the floor. When you are tired of your too faithful dog, of immovable stains on the curtains, of the regularity of meals, of sleeping in the same bed, of each action repeated every day, when you're tired of your self, of your own voice, of things ceaselessly repeating, of the narrow circle of your ideas, tired of the reflection seen in the mirror, of the appearance you make while shaving, whilst combing your hair, you must leave, start a new and unpredictable life.

Travel is a kind of door through which you leave behind your familiar existence and enter into an existence unexplored and dreamy.

A station! a port! a train whistling and spluttering its first jet of steam! A ship passing slowly through the harbour walls, its belly heaving with impatience, fleeing over there, to the horizon, towards new lands! Who can see that without quivering with envy, without feeling that stirring of desire in the soul for a long journey?

Everyone dreams of a favourite country, one person dreaming of Sweden, another of the Indies; this one of Greece, and that one of Japan. Myself, I was attracted, almost compelled, towards Africa by a yearning for the unknown Desert, attracted almost with a premonition that a passion was about to be born.

I left Paris on July 6, 1881. I wanted to see this land of sun and sand in full summer, under the heavy heat and in the furious glare of the light.

Everyone knows that splendid verse by the great poet Leconte de Lisle:

Midi, roi des étés, épandu sur la plaine,
Tombe, en nappes d'argent, des hauteurs du ciel bleu.
Tout se tait. L'air flamboie et brûle sans haleine;
La terre est assoupie en sa robe de feu.

[Noon, the king of summers, spread out over the plain,
Falling from the lofty blue sky in silver sheets.

Chapter One

All is silent. Without breath the air burns and flames,
Whilst the land, in its robe of fire, lays down and sleeps.] [4]

This is the noon of the desert, noon spread out over a sea of unmoving, boundless sand, the noon which made me leave those *flowered banks* of the Seine sung about by Madame Deshoulières [5]—the fresh bathing in the morning, the green shade of the woods—to traverse the blazing wilderness.

Algeria seemed particularly attractive at this time for another reason: the elusive Bou-Amama [6] was leading that fantastic campaign about which so many stupid things have been said and written. It was also asserted that the Muslim populations were preparing a general uprising, that they were going to have one last try, and that straight after Ramadan war would break out across Algeria. In this climate there was a growing curiosity to see the Arab, to try to comprehend that soul of his, something which the colonizers hardly worried about.

Flaubert sometimes said, 'You can visualize the desert, the pyramids, the Sphinx, before you set eyes upon them; but what you can't imagine is the head of a Turkish barber crouched in front of his door.' [7]

Wouldn't it be even more fascinating to know what goes on inside this head?

II

The Sea

Marseille flickers under the cheerful sun of a summer's day. She sparkles and beams with her cafés decked out in bunting, her horses capped with straw hats as though for a masquerade, and her people busy and noisy. She seems tipsy with her accent singing through the streets, that accent which everyone makes ring out like a challenge. Elsewhere a Marseillais is amusing, seeming to be a kind of foreigner, skinning the French tongue; but in Marseille, with all the Marseillais together, the accent is exaggerated to the extent it almost seems a joke. Everyone speaking like that, it's too much, a thunderous din![1] Marseille perspires under the sun like a beautiful girl who has let herself go, she smells like a dirty wench, smelling of garlic and a thousand other things. She smells of the innumerable foods nibbled on by the Negroes, Turks, Greeks, Italians, Maltese, Spanish, English, and Corsicans, she smells of the Marseillais too—those poor folk,[2] lying, sitting, rolling and sprawled out on the quays.

In le bassin de la Joliette,[3] the heavy liners are heating up, their noses turned towards the port entrance, they are covered with men loading them up with packages and merchandise.

One of them, the *Abd-el-Kader*,[4] all of a sudden begins to heave a low moan,— for the whistle is no longer used, having been replaced by a kind of animal cry—a formidable voice let rip from the fuming stomach of a monster.

The vast vessel leaves its moorings, passing slowly through the midst of its immobile brothers, it exits the port and, after the captain has brusquely thrown his command 'Full ahead' down into the depths of the boat via the megaphone, it thrusts forward with fervour into the open sea, leaving behind a long wake as it flees the coastline, Marseille disappearing into the horizon.

It's dinnertime on board. There are few people about, hardly anyone goes to Africa in July. At the end of the table are a colonel, an engineer, a doctor, and two middle-class gentlemen from Algiers with their wives.

They talk about the country they're heading to and the type of administration that it needs.

The Colonel emphatically calls for a military government, he talks of tactics in the desert, declaring that the telegraph is useless, even dangerous for the armies. This senior officer must have had some unpleasant war experiences through some fault of the telegraph.[5]

The engineer would like to entrust the colony to an inspector general of the Department of Civil Engineering[6] who would build canals, dams, roads and a thousand other things.

The captain of the boat let it be known, spiritedly, that a sailor would handle the matter better, what with Algeria only being accessible by sea.

The two middle-class gentlemen point out the crude faults of the governor;[7] and they both laugh, astonished that anyone can be so blundersome.

Going back on to the bridge, there is nothing but the sea, the calm sea, unstirring and gilded by the moon. The heavy boat seems to glide above it, leaving behind it a long, bubbling wake where the beaten water appears like liquid fire.

The bluish black sky spreads out above our heads, sown with stars that are at times veiled by the enormous plume of smoke spewed out by the chimney; and the little beacon at the top of the mast looks like a big star wandering amongst the others. Only the sound of the propeller in the depths of the ship can be heard. So charming are the evening hours passed on the bridge of a fleeing boat!

All day long next day, we lay thinking outstretched under the awning, the Ocean on all sides. Nightfall came and day duly followed. We had slept in narrow cabins on little coffin-shaped beds. It was now four o' clock in the morning, and I was up.

What an awakening! A lengthy coast and, directly opposite, a white spot growing bigger—Algiers!

III

Algiers

Unhoped for enchantment, delighting the Mind, Algiers exceeded all my expectations! So pretty, a town of snow under a dazzling light! An immense terrace skirts the port, held up by elegant arches. Above rise large European hotels and the French quarter, and beyond that the Arab town spreads out, a tangled mass of small, peculiar, white houses, separated by streets that are almost like underground passageways. The upper floors of the houses are borne up by series of white-painted posts and the roofs are adjoining. There are sudden openings into these inhabited dens, mysterious staircases towards dwellings that resemble burrows, teeming with Arab families. A woman passes, serious and veiled, her bare ankles—which are a little disconcerting—black from dust accumulated on sweat.

From the end of the jetty the view is marvellous. Full of wonder, you look at this cascade of sparkling houses running down one after the other from the top of the mountain to the sea. You might describe it as a torrent of foam, a mad froth of whiteness; and bubbling up from place to place a dazzling mosque, glimmering under the sun.

All around swarms an amazing populace. There are countless vagrants clothed in simple shirts, or two pieces of rug sewn together in an approximation of a tunic, or an old sack pierced with holes for the head and arms. Always barelegged and barefoot, they come and go, swearing, fighting with each other, verminous, ragged, caked in filth and stinking like animals.

Tartarin would say that they smack of the 'Teur' (Turk) and you can smell the Teur everywhere here.[1]

Then there is a whole world of dark-skinned kids, cross-breeds of Kabyles, Arabs, negroes and whites, an ants' nest of shoeshine boys, buzzing round like flies, leaping about, bold and vicious at three years of age, cunning as monkeys, they swear at you in Arabic and continue in French with their eternal '*cié mosieu*' ['shine, Sir']. They call you 'tu' and you call them 'tu'. Everyone here says 'Tu'. The coachman whom you stop in the street asks, 'Where will I take You [*Toi*]' which I point out to Parisian coachmen who are thus surpassed in their familiarity.

On the very same day as my arrival I saw an unimportant little event which nevertheless just about sums up the history of Algeria and colonization:

As I was sitting in front of a café, a young wog forcefully grabbed hold of my feet and began to wax them with great zest. After he had rubbed them for a quarter of an hour he returned my boots with their leather shining like a mirror, I gave him two sous.[2] '*Méci mosieu*' ['Thank you Sir'], he pronounced, but he didn't leave. He stayed crouched between my legs, completely motionless, rolling his eyes as if he was sick. I said to him: 'Get going, *arbico*.'[3] Still he didn't respond, still he didn't stir, then, all of a sudden, grabbing up in both his arms his box of waxes and polishes, he fled at full speed. And I noticed a big sixteen-year-old negro come out of a doorway, where he had been hiding, and pounce upon my shoeshine boy. In a few bounds he had caught up with him, then slapped him, searched him, tore from him the two sous, which he pocketed before calmly walking away, laughing, while the poor robbed boy howled in a frightful manner.

I was indignant, but my neighbour at the next table, an officer of Africa, a friend, said to me: 'Leave it be, it's the hierarchy that has been established. When they are not strong enough to take the money off others, they wax. But as soon as they feel in a position to duff the smallest ones, they do nothing else. They wait for the shoeshine boys and mug them.' Then, laughing, my companion added: 'Nearly everyone here does the same.'

The European quarter of Algiers, pretty from a distance, has, when seen close up, the appearance of a new town shoved under an unsuitable climate. On disembarking, a large sign catches your eye: 'Algiers Skating Rink'; and for the first few steps, one is caught up and left embarrassed by the badly applied sense of progress here, by the brutal, warped civilization that has so little adapted itself to the morals [*moeurs*], climate and people of this land. It is us who appear barbarous in the midst of these barbarians; yes, it's true, they may be crude, but it's their home, and over the centuries they have learnt customs of which, it seems, we are yet to understand the meaning.

Napoléon III had a wise word to say on the subject (perhaps whispered to him by a minister): 'What Algeria needs is not conquerors, but initiators'.[4] However, we have remained brutal conquerors, tactless and obsessed by our preconceived ideas. We have planted our morals [*moeurs*], our Parisian-style houses, and our offensive habits on this soil, like tasteless art, like people lacking in wisdom or understanding. Everything we do seems to be a misinterpretation, a challenge to this country, not so much to her first inhabitants, as to the very earth itself.

A few days after my arrival I witnessed an open-air ball in Mustapha.[5] It was like the fair at Neuilly.[6] There were gingerbread stalls, shooting galleries, tombolas, clay pipe shooting, fortune-tellers, mermaids,[7] draper's assistants dancing real Bullier-style quadrilles[8] with shop girls, whilst behind the enclosure where one paid to enter, out in the broad, sandy plain of the parade ground, hundreds of Arabs were lying down under the moon, motionless in their white rags, listening gravely to the refrains of the *chahuts*[9] got up by the French.

IV

The Province of Oran [1]

It's one day by rail to get from Algiers to Oran. First you cross the fertile, shady and populated plain of Mitidja, which is what is shown to a new arrival to prove to him the fertility of our colony. The Mitidja and Kabylie are certainly two admirable regions. [2] Kabylie is actually more densely populated per square kilometre than the Pas-de-Calais, [3] and the Mitidja will soon be as much. So what exactly is meant to be colonized there you might ask? I will come back to this subject later.

The train rolls forwards and the cultivated plains disappear, the earth becoming bare and red, the real earth of Africa. The horizon widens, a sterile and burning horizon. We follow the immense Chélif valley, enclosed by desolate, grey, scorched mountains, without trees, without grass. Here and there the mountain chain drops, half-opens to better show the awful misery of the soil devastated by the sun. A vast, completely flat area unfolds, bounded over there by a nearly invisible line of hilltops lost in a haze. Sometimes on the uncultivated ridges, big white spots appear, like enormous eggs laid there by giant birds. They are marabouts raised in praise of Allah. [4]

An interminable yellow plain, sometimes you see a clump of trees and some men standing about—tanned Europeans, big in stature—watching the train fly past. Close by are little tents, like fat mushrooms, out of which go bearded soldiers. It's a hamlet of farmers protected by a line detachment.

In this expanse of sterile and dusty land you notice, so far away that you can barely see it, a sort of smoke, a thin cloud which rises towards the sky and seems to run straight across the soil. It's a horseman kicking up under the feet of his horse the fine, scorched dust. And each one of these clouds on the plain indicates a man whose light, almost imperceptible burnous you eventually discern.[5]

From time to time there are native camps, and these *douars*[6] are barely discernible, situated close to a dried out stream where some children take a few goats, sheep, or cows to graze (though the word 'graze' here seems infinitely risible). Their huts are made out of brown canvas and, surrounded by dry undergrowth, they merge in with the monotonous colour of the earth. On the embankment of the railway line a man with black skin, bare wiry legs with no calves, and wrapped up in whitish rags, gravely contemplates the iron beast which passes in front of him.

Further along a troop of nomads is on the move. The caravan advances through the dust leaving a cloud behind it. The women and children are mounted on asses or little horses; whilst the riders at the front move forward solemnly, at an infinitely noble pace.

And it is always like that. A European village is revealed every now and then when the train stops: a few houses similar to those of Nanterre or Rueil,[7] a few burnt trees, around which are draped tricolores, for July 14, a serious-looking gendarme in front of the station exit, seeming also just like a gendarme of Rueil or Nanterre.

The heat is unbearable. All metal objects become impossible to touch, even inside the carriage. The water from the flasks burns your mouth. The air that rushes through the carriage door seems to be blown from the mouth of a furnace. In Orléansville the station thermometer reads over forty-nine degrees in the shade!

We arrive in Oran for dinner.

Oran is a true European town, commercial, more Spanish than French, and of no special interest. On the streets you encounter beautiful girls with black eyes, ivory skin and bright teeth. When the weather's nice it appears you can see the Spanish coasts on the horizon, their fatherland.

As soon as you step on to African soil, a strange desire takes a hold of you, the wont to go further, to go south.

And so with a ticket to Saïda, I took the little narrow gauge railway that climbs through the hauts plateaux.[8] Around this town the elusive Bou-Amama and his horsemen prowled.

The Province of Oran

A few hours down the line we reach the first slopes of the Atlas [mountains].[9] The train climbs, puffing, scarcely moving, snaking along the flanks of the arid hills. It passes an immense lake formed by three rivers and amassed in three valleys, guarded over by the famous Habra dam. A colossal wall five hundred metres long contains, suspended above a vast plain, fourteen million cubic metres of water.

(This dam collapsed the following year, drowning hundreds of men and ruining an entire country. At the time the nation was concerned with collecting for the flooded Hungarians or Spanish. No one cared about this French disaster.) [10]

Next we go through a narrow pass between two mountains which could be described as suffering from recent burns, so red and raw was their skin; we bypass peaks and spin alongside the slopes, making diversions of ten kilometres to avoid obstacles, then we rush into a plain at full speed, always zig-zagging a bit, as if in continuation of the habit.

The carriages are very small, the engine fat like that of a tramway. Sometimes she seems exhausted, rattling, whining, or raging, and going so slowly you could follow it on foot, then suddenly she sets off at a fury.

The whole region is arid and desolate. The King of Africa, the Sun, the great and ferocious ravager, has eaten the flesh of these valleys, leaving behind only stone and a red dust where nothing can grow.

Saïda! It's a small French town which seems to be inhabited only by generals. There are at least ten or twelve, and they appear to always be in consultation. You have a mind to shout to them: 'Where is Bou-Amama today, my general?' The civilian population has no respect for the uniform.

The hostelry here leaves a lot to be desired, I sleep on a straw mattress in a room bleached with lime. The heat is unbearable; I close my eyes to sleep. If only!

My window is open, looking out on to a little courtyard. I hear the barking of dogs. They are far away, very far away, and yapping in fits and starts as they answer each other.

But soon they're approaching, coming nearer; now they're there right up by the houses, in the vines, in the streets. They're there, five hundred of them, perhaps a thousand, starving and ferocious, they are the dogs who guarded the Spanish camps on the hauts plateaux. Their masters killed or gone, the beasts prowled, dying of hunger; then they found the town, and they surrounded it, like an army.

In the day they sleep in the ravines under rocks, in dens in the mountains; as soon as night falls they arrive in Saïda to search for a means of survival.

Men returning home late walk with revolvers in their fists, as they are nosed out and followed by twenty or thirty yellowish dogs, similar to foxes.

At present they are barking continually, in a frightful manner that is enough to drive you mad. Then other cries start up, high-pitched yelpings; these are the jackals arriving; sometimes you hear only one voice, strong and singular, that of the hyena, which imitates dogs in order to attract and devour them.

This horrible din lasts without respite until day.

Before the French occupation Saïda was protected by a small fortress built by Abd-el-Kader.[11]

The new town is in a depression, surrounded by exposed heights. A river thin enough to almost jump across waters the surrounding fields where beautiful vines grow.

Towards the south, the neighbouring hills have the appearance of a high defensive wall, they are the last tiers leading up to the hauts plateaux.

On the left stands a rock, blazing red in colour, about fifty metres high and which has on its summit a few stone-works in ruins. It's all that remains of the Saïda of Abd-el-Kader. Seen from afar, this rock seems to adhere to the mountain, but if you climb it, you will rest full of surprise and admiration: a deep ravine dug between completely straight walls separates the old redoubt of the emir from the neighbouring hill. This hill is of crimson stone and is nicked and notched in places where the winter rains fall. Down in the ravine the river runs in the midst of a wood of oleander. From up high you might say it looked like an Oriental rug spread out in a corridor. The blanket of flowers appears uninterrupted, mottled only by the green foliage which breaks through in places.

One goes down into this valley by a path better suited to goats.

The river or stream down there (the Oued Saïda),[12] a brook to us, splashes against the stones beneath the big shrubs in full bloom, it jumps over rocks, froths, ripples and murmurs. The water is hot, almost boiling. Enormous crabs run along the banks at a peculiar speed, their pincers raised on seeing me. Fat green lizards disappear into the foliage. Sometimes a serpent slips between the boulders.

The ravine narrows as if it were going to close in on itself. A great noise overhead makes me tremble. An eagle, surprised, flies away from its haunt, rising up towards the blue sky, climbing with slow and strong wing beats, wings so broad that they seem to touch both walls.

After an hour the path rejoins the road which climbs the dusty mount going towards Aïn-el-Hadjar.

In front of me a woman walks along, an old woman in a black skirt, capped in a white bonnet, stooped, with a basket under her left arm, and holding in the other a kind of sunshade, a huge red parasol. A woman here! A country-woman here in this dismal region where one sees nothing but the tall negress, arched, glossy, bedecked in yellow, blue or red fabrics, and who in passing leaves an aroma of human flesh that is enough to turn the most solid of hearts.[13]

The old woman, exhausted, sits down in the dust, panting in the torrid heat. She has a face wrinkled by innumerable little pleats of skin, like the gathers in fabrics, a weary appearance, overwhelmed, despairing.

I spoke to her. She was an Alsatian who had been sent to this desolate country with her four sons after the war.[14] She said to me:

'You come from over there?'

This 'over there' pulled at my heart.

'Yes.'

And she began to cry. Then she told me her story very simply.

They had been promised land. They came, the mother and children. Now three of her sons were dead from this murdering climate. Only one remained, who was ill. Their fields, although large, did not return anything, for they hadn't a drop of water. 'Of cinders, Sir, of burnt cinders', the old woman repeated. 'They can't produce a cabbage, not a cabbage, not even a cabbage!' she said, persevering with this cabbage idea which must represent for her all terrestrial happiness.

I have never seen anything more distressing than this good woman of Alsace thrown on to a soil of fire where not even a cabbage grows. How she must often think of that lost country, of the green countryside of her youth, the poor old woman!

On leaving, she added, 'Do you know if they are giving out land in Tunisia?[15] They say it's good there. It's got to be better than here. And then perhaps I could get my boy to recover there.'

All our colonists installed beyond the Tell could say something similar.[16]

A desire always takes hold of me, a desire to go further. But the country was in a state of war, I couldn't risk going alone. An opportunity arose, a train was going to resupply the troops camped along the chotts. [17]

It was one of the sirocco's days. [18] Since the morning the south wind had got up, blowing over the land in slow, heavy, devouring breaths. At seven o' clock the little convoy set off, carrying two detachments of infantry with their officers, three tank cars full of water, and the engineers of the company, because for three weeks no train had gone to those ends of the line that the Arabs could destroy.

The engine 'L'Hyène' [the *Hyena*] leaves noisily, advancing straight towards the mountain as if she wanted to smash through it. Then suddenly she makes a curve, plunging into a narrow valley, hooking round, and returning to pass fifty metres above the place where she was running just before. She turns anew, tracing circuits, one after the other, climbing always in zig-zags, unwinding like a big lace on her way to reaching the summit of the mount.

Here there are some vast buildings, chimneys of factories, a sort of little ghost town. These are the splendid factories of the Franco-Algerian Company. [19] Esparto was prepared there before the massacre of the Spanish. [20] The place is called Aïn-el-Hadjar.

We are still climbing. The locomotive blows, rattles, slows down, stops. Three times she tries to set off again, three times she remains powerless. She backs up to gain momentum, but still remains without power in the middle of the too arduous slope.

And so the officers make the soldiers get off and they pop out the length of the train and begin to push. We set off again slowly, at a walking pace. Laughing and jesting; the infantrymen make fun of the engine. It's finished. We are here on the hauts plateaux.

The mechanic, his body leaning outside, ceaselessly looks at the track in case it's been cut up; and the rest of us inspect the horizon attentively, on the alert since a small column of dust seems to indicate in the distance an as yet invisible horseman. We carry rifles and revolvers.

Sometimes a jackal flees in front of us; a huge vulture flies away, abandoning the carcass of a camel almost entirely picked to pieces; Carthaginian hens [*poules de Carthage*], [21] very similar to partridges, escape to clusters of dwarf palm trees.

At the little station of Tafraoua two line companies are camped. A lot of Spaniards were killed here.

The Province of Oran

At Kralfallah there's a company of Zouaves [22] fortifying themselves hastily, building their entrenchments with rails, beams, telegraph posts, balls of esparto, anything they can find. We lunch there, the three officers—the captain, the lieutenant and the sub-lieutenant—all very young and cheerful, inviting us to the café.

The train sets off again. It runs interminably through a boundless plain which, with its tufts of esparto, is made to resemble a calm sea. The sirocco becomes intolerable, throwing in our faces the enflamed air of the desert; and sometimes on the horizon a vague form appears. You might say it looked like a lake with an island, some rocks in the water: it's the mirage. On the embankment there are some scorched rocks and some human bones: the remains of a Spaniard. Elsewhere, dead camels, always picked apart by vultures.

We traverse a forest! What a forest! An ocean of sand where the rare tufts of juniper resemble lettuce seedlings in a gigantic kitchen garden! From now on there's no greenery, except the esparto, a type of blue-green rush which sprouts in round tufts and covers the ground as far as the eye can see.

Sometimes you think you see a horseman in the distance. But he disappears and perhaps you've been mistaken.

We arrive at the Oued-Fallette in the middle of a completely gloomy and deserted area. I go for a little walk with two companions, still heading south. We climb a low hill under a crushing heat. The sirocco hauls fire; it dries the sweat on your face as soon as it appears, burns your lips and eyes, dries your throat. Scorpions are found under all the stones.

Around the stationary train—which from afar has the appearance of a big, black beast laid down upon the dry earth—the soldiers load the vehicles sent from a neighbouring camp.

Then they move off in the dust, slowly, their pace weighed down under the crushing sun. For a long, long time we can see them going over there to the left; then we can only see the grey cloud that they raise above them.

Six of us stay near the train. You can't touch anything, everything burns. The copper-plate of the coaches seems reddened with fire. You cry out if your hand touches the steel of the weapons.

It was here a few days ago that the rebelling Rezaïna tribe crossed the chott we could not reach (the hour forcing us to return). The heat was such during their passage across this desiccated marsh that the fugitive tribe lost all their donkeys from thirst, and even sixteen children, who died in the arms of their mothers.

The engine whistles. We leave the Oued-Fallette. A remarkable act of war made this place famous throughout the region.

A column was established there, kept by a detachment of the 15th line. Now, one night, after a ten hour ride, two *goumiers*[23] presented themselves at the outposts carrying a pressing order from the major general at Saïda. In accordance with custom, they waved a torch in order to be recognized. The sentinel, a recruit newly arrived from France, ignoring the customs and the rules of service in the southern region—and by no means prevented by his officers—fired at the couriers. The poor devils came forward nevertheless; the sentry took up their weapons; the men got into position, and a terrible gunfire began. After having endured a hundred and fifty shots of gunfire, the two Arabs finally withdrew; one of them with a bullet in his shoulder. The following day they returned to headquarters, returning their dispatches.

V

Bou-Amama

Even today they describe him as extremely cunning, the one known as Bou-Amama. This elusive joker, after having thrown our African army into disarray, disappeared so completely you began to wonder whether he had ever existed.

Trustworthy officers who believed they knew him described him to me in one way, but other no less honest people, certain to have seen him, painted him to me in different colours.

In all cases, this prowler was the head of only a small band of men, doubtless pushed to revolt by the famine. These people fought only to empty silos or plunder convoys. They seem to have acted not out of hatred or religious fanaticism, but out of hunger. And with our system of colonization consisting of ruining the Arab, fleecing him without respite, pursuing him without mercy, and making him destitute, we are going to see more uprisings.

Perhaps another reason for this campaign is the presence of the Spanish esparto farmers on the hauts plateaux.

In this ocean of esparto, in this dull, greenish expanse, unmoving under an incendiary sky, lived a true nation, hoards of men with brown skin, mercenaries that had been driven out of their homeland by extreme poverty and other such reasons. Wilder and more feared than the Arabs, thus isolated, far from any town, any law, any force, they did, it's said, what their ancestors did in new lands: they were terrible, bloodthirsty, and violent towards the primitive inhabitants.

The vengeance of the Arabs was horrendous.

And there in a few lines you have the apparent origin of the uprising.

Two marabouts[1] were openly preaching revolt amongst a tribe from the South. Lieutenant Weinbrenner[2] was dispatched with the mission to capture the *caïd* of this tribe.[3] The French officer had an escort of *four* men. He was assassinated.

Colonel Innocenti[4] was instructed to avenge this death, and they sent him backing in the form of the agha of Saïda.[5]

However, en route, the agha of Saïda's *goum* met the Trafis who were also going to meet up with Colonel Innocenti. Arguments broke out between the two tribes; the Trafis defected and went to place themselves at the disposal of Bou-Amama. And then the Chellala incident that has been told a hundred times before took place.[6] After the sacking of his convoy, Colonel Innocenti, who public opinion seems to have let off somewhat lightly, continued with forced marches towards le Kreïder, in order to regroup his column, leaving the road entirely open to his adversary, who duly profited from this.

Let us make note of a curious incident. On the same day, the official dispatches signalled that Bou-Amama was in two different places at the same time, two points one hundred and fifty kilometres apart.

This chief, profiting from the great liberty that was given to him, came within twelve kilometres of Géryville, killing on the way Brigadier Bringeard, who had been sent into this land of open revolt with only a few men to establish telegraphic communications; Bou-Amama then continued northwards.

And so he crossed the territory of the Hassassenas and the Harrars, and he probably gave orders to these two tribes for the general massacre of the Spanish, which they were to carry out a little afterwards.

Finally he arrived at Aïn-Kétifa, and two days later he was camping at Haci-Tirsine, only twenty-two kilometres from Saïda.

On the evening of June 10th the military authorities, at last anxious, gave the Franco-Algerian Company notice to make all of its agents return, the region being unsafe. Trains ran all night to the ends of the line; but in just a few hours they couldn't hook up with all the worksites spread out over a territory of one hundred and fifty kilometres, and on the eleventh, at the break of day, the massacres began.

They were carried out mostly by the Hassassenas and Harrars tribes, exasperated with the Spanish who were living on their territories.

But, under the pretext of not pushing them again to revolt, these tribes who slit the throats of nearly three hundred men, women, and children, have been left in peace. Arab horsemen found with packs laden with plunder, the dresses of Spanish women under their saddles, were released, so it goes, on the grounds that there wasn't enough evidence.

So, on the evening of the 10th, Bou-Amama was encamped at Haci-Tirsine, twenty-two kilometres from Saïda. At the same time, General Cérez [7] was telegraphing to the governor that the rebel leader was endeavouring to head back south.

In the following days the hardy marabout pillaged the villages of Tafraoua and Kralfallah, loading all his camels with loot, carrying away goods and provisions to the value of several millions.

He went back once more to Haci-Tirsine to reconvene his troops; then he divided his convoy into two parts, one of which headed towards Aïn-Kétifa, where it was stopped and pillaged by the *goum* de Sharraouï (Brunetière column). [8]

The other section, commanded by Bou-Amama himself, found itself caught between the column of General Détrie, camped at El-Maya, and the Mallaret column, [10] posted not far from [le] Kreïder, at Ksar-el-Krelifa. It had to pass between the two, which wasn't going to be easy. Bou-Amama therefore sent a party of horsemen out in front of the camp of General Détrie [9] who followed them with his whole column as far as Aïn-Sfisifa, well beyond the Chott, persuaded that he had the marabout [Bou-Amama] in front of him. The ruse was a success. The path was clear. The following day, the 14th June, following the departure of the General, the rebel chief occupied his camp.

For his part, Colonel Mallaret, instead of watching the passage to [le] Kreïder, was camped at Ksar-el-Krelifa, four kilometres away. Bou-Amama at once sent a strong detachment of horsemen to defilade in front of the Colonel, who contented himself with firing six mythical cannon shots. And, during this time, the convoy of laden camels peacefully passed over the chott to [le] Kreïder, at the only point where the crossing was easy. From there the marabout went to place his provisions in the care of his tribe, the Mogrars, four hundred kilometres south of Géryville.

Where do these precise details come from, you might ask? Well, from everyone. Naturally some points are contested by some, and other points by others. I cannot affirm anything, having done nothing but set down the information that seems to me the most probable. Besides, it's impossible in Algeria to obtain exact details about what happened, even if what happened happened only three kilometres from the place where you find yourself. As for the military news, throughout this countryside it seemed to be provided by practical jokers. On the same day, Bou-Amama was sighted at six different points by six heads of corps who believed they beheld him. A complete collection of official dispatches with a little supplement containing those from authorized agencies would make up a wholly amusing anthology. Certain dispatches, whose improbability is all too evident, were besides blocked in the offices in Algiers.

A witty caricature done by a colonist summed up the situation for me. It showed an old fat moustachioed general with his stripes, standing opposite the desert. He casts a worried eye over the immense, bare and undulating country, the limits of which he cannot perceive, and murmers: 'They are there!...somewhere!' Then addressing his aide-de-camp, without turning around, he pronounces in a firm voice: 'Telegraph the government that the enemy is in front of me and that I'm beginning pursuit.'

The only information of which one can be a little bit certain is that obtained from the Spanish prisoners who escaped from Bou-Amama. I was able to converse, by means of an interpreter, with one of these men, and here is what he told me.

He was named Blas Rojo Pélisaire. On the evening of June 10th, he was driving a convoy of seven carts with his comrades when they found on the road some broken carts and, between the wheels, the massacred carters. One of them was still alive. They began to attend to him; but a troop of Arabs jumped upon them. The Spaniards only had one gun; they surrendered; they were massacred nevertheless, with the exception of Blas Rojo, without doubt spared because of his youth and pleasing mien. It's known that the Arabs are not at all indifferent to the beauty of men. They took him to their camp where he found other prisoners. At midnight they killed one of them without reason. He was a *mechanic* (one of those responsible for tightening the carts' brakes) named Domingo.

The following day, the 11th, Blas learnt that other prisoners had been killed in the night. It was the day of the big massacres. They remained in the same place; then, in the evening, the horsemen brought in two women and a child.

The 12th, they pack up the camp and walk all day.

The 13th, in the evening they camped at Dayat-Kereb.

Bou-Amama

The 14th, they walk in the direction of Ksar-[el-]Krelifa. It's the day of the Mallaret affair. The prisoner didn't hear the cannon. This leaves us to suppose that Bou-Amama made a party of horsemen defilade only in front of the expeditionary French corps, whilst the booty convoy, in which Blas found himself, passed over the chott a few kilometres further on, well under cover.

For eight hours they walked in zig-zags. When they arrived at Tis-Moulins the dissident tribes separated, each taking with them their prisoners.

Bou-Amama acted benevolently to the prisoners, especially to the women, whom he put to bed in a specially guarded tent.

One of them, a beautiful eighteen-year-old girl, was married en route to a Trafi chief who had threatened her with death if she resisted. But the marabout [Bou-Amama] refused to consecrate their union.

Blas Rojo was attached to the service of Bou-Amama, whom, however, he did not see. He only saw his son, who directed the military operations. He seemed to be about thirty years of age. He was a tall, lean, pale brown boy with large eyes, sporting a small beard.[11]

He possessed two chestnut horses, one of which was French and seemed to have belonged to Commander Jacquet. The prisoner had no knowledge of the [le] Kreïder affair.

Blas Rojo ran away in the environs of Bas-Yala, but not knowing the country well, he was forced to follow dried out rivers, and after three days and nights of walking he arrived at Marhoum. Bou-Amama had with him five hundred horsemen and three hundred infantrymen, plus a convoy of camels to carry the booty.

Trains ran day and night on the little railway of the chotts during the fortnight after the massacres. They constantly picked up mutilated and abject Spaniards, large numbers of beautiful naked girls, violated and blood-stained. The military authority could have avoided this butchery with a little foresight, say all the inhabitants of the region. What it could not do, in these instances, was stamp out a handful of rebels. What are the reasons for the ineffectiveness of our superior weaponry against the bludgeons and muskets of the Arabs? It's for others to examine and point them out.

The Arabs, in any case, have an advantage over us, which we can only try in vain to overcome. They are the sons of the country. Surviving on a few figs and a few grains of meal, indefatigable in this climate which exhausts the men from the

North, mounted on horses temperate like them and insensitive to the heat like them, they can cover in one day a hundred or a hundred and thirty kilometres. Having neither baggage, nor convoys, nor provisions to trail behind them, they move about with a surprising rapidity, passing between two encamped columns to attack and pillage a village which was believed to be secure, disappearing without leaving a trace, then returning abruptly when they were thought to be far away.

In European warfare, whatever the promptitude of a marching army, it can't move about without someone being informed. The mass of baggage fatally slows down movements and always indicates the road followed. An Arab party, on the contrary, leaves no more traces of its passage than the flight of a bird. These wandering horsemen come and go about us with the darting celerity of swallows.

When they attack, they can be overcome, and nearly always beaten, in spite of their courage. But they cannot be pursued, you can never catch up with them when they flee. What's more, they carefully avoid encounters, and in general content themselves with hassling our troops. They charge with impetuosity, at a furious gallop on their lean horses, arriving like a storm of floating linen and dust.

Galloping all the while, they discharge their long, damascened rifles, then, suddenly describing a brusque arc, they move away as quickly as they came, stomach to the ground, from place to place leaving on the soil behind them an agitated white bundle, fallen there like a wounded bird with blood on its feathers.

VI

The Province of Algiers

The *Algériens*, that is the inhabitants of Algiers,¹ know little more of their country than the plain of Mitidja. They live peacefully in one of the most adorable towns in the world, declaring that the Arabs are an ungovernable people, only fit to be killed or thrown back into the desert.

Moreover, when it comes to Arabs, they have only seen the lowlife from the south which swarms about their streets. In the cafés there is talk of Laghouat, Bou-Saada, and Saïda as if these places were on the other side of the world. It's very seldom that an officer comes to know all three provinces. He nearly always remains in the same area until the time when he returns to France.

It's pertinent to add that travelling becomes very difficult as soon as you venture outside the well-known roads in the south. You can only do so with the support and obligingness of the military authorities. The commanders of advanced areas regard themselves as veritable omnipotent monarchs; and no unknown person could chance to cross their lands without great risk... from the Arabs. Any isolated man would immediately be stopped by the *caïds*, led under escort to the closest officer, and brought back between two spahis to civilian territory.²

But as soon as you can present the least recommendation, you meet with, on the part of the officers from the *bureaux arabes*,³ all conceivable good grace. Living alone, so far from any neighbours, they welcome the traveller in the most charming manner; living alone, they read a lot, they are informed, educated and converse with pleasure; living alone in this broad, desolate land with its never-ending horizons, they know how to think like solitary workers. Having left with the prejudices generally held in France against these *bureaux*, I returned with ideas much to the contrary.

It's thanks to several of these officers that I could make a long excursion outside of the well-known roads, going from tribe to tribe.

Ramadan had just begun. There was anxiety in the colony for it was feared that there would be a general insurrection when this Mohammedan Lent was over.

Ramadan lasts thirty days. During this period no follower of Mohammed can drink, eat or smoke from when the sun appears in the morning till the hour when the eye cannot distinguish between *a white thread and a red thread*.[4] This tough regulation is not followed absolutely to the letter, and you see more than one cigarette lit as soon as the fiery star hides itself behind the horizon, but before you can cease to distinguish the red or black colour of a thread.

Apart from this regulation concerning smoking, no Arab transgresses the severe law of the fast of absolute abstinence. Men, women, boys from the age of fifteen, and girls as soon as they are of marrying age, that's to say between eleven and thirteen or thereabouts, spend the entire day without either eating or drinking. Not eating is nothing; but abstaining from drinking is horrible because of the frightful heat. In this Lent there is no exemption. What's more, nobody would dare to ask for it; and even the whores themselves, the Oulad-Naïl[5] who swarm about in all the Arab centres and big oases, fast just the same as the marabouts, perhaps even more than the marabouts. And those Arabs that one believed to be civilized, that showed themselves in ordinary times to be disposed to accept our morals [*moeurs*], share our ideas and support our action, suddenly revert, as soon as Ramadan begins, to being wildly fanatical and stupidly fervent.

It is easy to understand what furious exaltation results from this tough religious practice on these narrow-minded and obstinate intellects. All day these unfortunate people meditate, stomachs rumbling, watching the conquering *roumis*[6] pass by eating, drinking and smoking in front of them. And they repeat to themselves that if they kill one of these *roumis* during Ramadan, they will go straight to heaven, and that the era of our domination is reaching its end, for their marabouts ceaselessly promise them that they are going to drive us all into the sea with bludgeon blows.

It's during Ramadan in particular that the Aïssaouas[7] come to the fore, these religious showmen who eat scorpions and swallow snakes are the only ones, perhaps with a few misbelievers and a few noblemen, who do not have a violent faith [in adhering to the fast of Ramadan].

These exceptions are infinitely rare; I am only able to cite one.

On leaving for a twenty day's march in the South, an officer of the Boghar circle asked three spahis who were accompanying him to not do Ramadan, calculating that he wouldn't be able to achieve anything with these men exhausted from fasting. Two of the soldiers refused, the third replied: 'Lieutenant, I don't do Ramadan. I'm not a marabout, me, I'm a noble.'

He was, in fact, *de grande tente* [Maupassant's italics],[8] a son of one of the oldest and most illustrious families of the desert.

A strange custom persists, which dates back to the occupation, and which seems profoundly absurd when you think over the awful results Ramadan can have for us. It was thought to begin with that the best way to conciliate the vanquished was to flatter their religion. And so it was decided that the French cannon would give the signal for abstinence during the holy period. And so each morning, with the first redness of dawn, a cannon shot orders the fast; and, each evening, about twenty minutes after the sun has set, across all the towns, forts, and *places militaires*,[9] another cannon shot is fired, leading to the lighting up of thousands of cigarettes, to thousands drinking from water jugs and to the preparation of innumerable dishes of couscous across Algeria.

I was able to attend the Grand Mosque at Algiers[10] for the religious ceremony which opened Ramadan.

The structure is very simple, with walls bleached with lime, and the floor covered with a thick carpet. The Arabs enter sharply, barefooted, with their shoes in their hands. They position themselves in long uniform lines, which are on the whole spaced out with greater regularity than rows of soldiers at exercises. They place their shoes and the other small objects they have in their hands on the ground in front of them; and they remain still like statues, faces turned towards a little chapel which indicates the direction of Mecca.

In this chapel is the official mufti.[11] His old, soft, plaintive and very monotonous voice wails a kind of sad chant which, heard once, you never forget. The intonation often changes, and then those attending him, in one rhythmic, silent and prompt movement, touch their foreheads on the ground, staying prostrate for a few seconds and getting up without making a noise, without anything obscuring for a second the little, trembling chant of the mufti. Unceasingly the whole congregation thus falls down and gets back up again with fantastic promptness, silence and regularity. The din of chairs, coughs and whispers found in a Catholic church is not heard in there. It feels as though these people have been filled with a plain, wild faith, bending and straightening them like puppets; a dumb and tyrannical faith invading bodies, immobilizing faces and twisting hearts. An indefinable feeling of respect mixed with pity takes a hold of you in the face of these lean fanatics who no longer have any stomach to hinder their supple prostrations, and who carry out their religion with the mechanism and rectitude of Prussian soldiers doing manoeuvres.

The walls are white, the rugs on the ground are red; the men are white, red, blue or other colours, according to the fancy of their pageantry clothing, which they wear loosely draped but with proud bearing, their heads and shoulders bathing in the soft light falling from the chandeliers.

A group of marabouts occupy a platform and sing the response with the same intonation of head directed by the mufti. And so it continues indefinitely.

It's during the evenings of Ramadan that you should visit the Casbah.[12] This title of Casbah, which means citadel, has ended up designating the entire Arab town. Since one fasts and sleeps in the day, one eats and lives at night. And the little steep streets—like mountain paths, or runs dug by animals, uneven and narrow, continually turning, crossing and muddling up with each other, and so profoundly mysterious that in spite of yourself you speak in hushed tones there—are traversed by a population out of *The Thousand and One Nights*. That's exactly the impression you feel there, that you are taking a trip in the land which Sultana Scheherazade narrated to us.[13] There are low doors with admirable trappings, as thick as prison walls; there are veiled women; in the depth of the half-open courtyards faces momentarily appear, and then there are all those vague noises at the back of the houses which are closed up like treasure troves. Often, on the doorsteps men are stretched out, eating and drinking. Sometimes the sprawled out groups take up the whole narrow passageway. You have to step over naked calves, brush against hands, be careful where you put your feet in the midst of bundles of white, outspread linen from which protrude heads and limbs.

The Jews keep open dens which serve them as shops; and clandestine houses of pleasure, full of clamour, are so numerous that you can't walk five minutes without coming across two or three.

The Province of Algiers

In the Arab cafés groups of men packed up one against the other, squatting on benches that are stuck to the walls, or simply sitting on the ground, drink coffee out of microscopic receptacles. They are motionless and mute, holding their cups in their hands, every so often raising them to their mouths in extremely slow movements, and a space in which ten of us would feel crowded can hold twenty of them, so packed in are they.

And the fanatics have a calm appearance, coming and going in the midst of these tranquil drinkers, preaching revolt, announcing the end of servitude.

It's said of the *ksar* (an Arab village) of Boukhrari that it always produces the first symptoms of big insurrections. This village is found on the road to Laghouat. Let's go there.

Looking at the Atlas [Mountains] from the immense Mitidja Plain, you see a gigantic cutting which splits the mountains in the direction of the south, as though a blow from an axe has opened it up. This perforation is called the Chiffa gorge and through it goes the road for Médéah, Boukhrari and Laghouat.

Following the thin river Chiffa, you enter into the cutting of the mountain, sinking deep into the narrow, wild and woody gorge.

There are springs everywhere. Trees climb up the sheer rock faces, they cling everywhere, as though mounting an escalade.

The passage contracts further. The upright rocks threaten you; the sky appears like a blue band between the summits; then suddenly, in an abrupt turning, at the beginning of a ravine covered with trees, a little inn reveals itself. It's the Auberge du *Ruisseau-des-Singes*.[14]

In front of the door, the water sings in the ponds; it springs forth and falls back down, filling this corner with freshness, making you think of calm little Swiss valleys. You rest, doze off in the shade; then all of a sudden, above your head, a branch stirs; you get up—and throughout the dense foliage monkeys are fleeing headlong with leaps, tumbles, jumps and cries.

There are hundreds of them, thousands perhaps, ranging from the very small to the enormous. The wood is full of them, swarming and populous. Some of them, captured by the owners of the inn, are affectionate and placid. One, taken the other week and still very young, remains a little wild.

When you stay still, they approach you, watch over and observe you. You could say that the traveller is a great amusement for the inhabitants of this valley.

On certain days, however, you won't see a single one of them.

After the Auberge du *Ruisseau-des-Singes*, the path constricts itself once more; then suddenly, on the left, two big waterfalls shoot forth near the summit of the mountain, two clear waterfalls, two silver ribbons. If you only knew how sweet a sight these waterfalls are on African land! We climb for a long, long time. The gorge is less deep, less wooded. Still climbing, the mountain becomes denuded little by little. There are fields now; and when we reach the ridge, we meet oaks, willows and young elms, the trees of our country. We spend the night at Médéah, a little white village very similar to a sub-prefecture of France.

After Médéah the ferocious ravages of the sun begin again. Again we cross a forest, but a meagre forest, threadbare and showing everywhere the burnt skin of the soon vanquished land. Soon there's no longer any sign of life around us.

On my left a valley opens up, red, dry, and not a blade of grass; it stretches into the distance, like a basin of sand. Suddenly a big shadow crosses it. It passes from one end to the other, a flying stain that slips over the naked soil. This shadow is the true and only inhabitant of this dead and desolate place. It seems to reign here like a mysterious and deadly spirit.

I raise my eyes and spot it passing with wings outstretched and motionless, that great cutter-up of carcasses, the lean vulture gliding over his domain, below the other master that kills this vast land, the sun, the hard sun.

When you descend towards Boukhrari, you are confronted with, for as far as the eye can see, the interminable Chélif valley. There in all its hideousness and poverty, the yellow poverty of the earth is revealed. This valley through which runs the dirty rut of a stream without water, drunk to its muddy dregs by the fire of the sky, this valley is dressed in tatters like a poor old Arab. This time the fire which replaces the air and fills the horizon has conquered, devoured, and pulverized everything.

Something passes over your brow: elsewhere it would be the wind, but here it is fire. Something floats over there on the stony crests: elsewhere it would be a mist, but here it is fire, or moreover the heat made visible. If the soil wasn't already bone dry, this strange steam would remind you of the little wisps of smoke that rise from living flesh burnt with a red hot iron. And everything has a strange colour, blinding yet velvety. The colour of the hot sand seems to be mixed with a purplish shade, fallen molten from the sky.

The Province of Algiers

There aren't any insects in this dusty earth. Only a few big ants. The thousand little beings that you see at home would not be able to live in this furnace. On certain torrid days even the flies die, like when the cold weather returns in the North. And it's hardly worth rearing chickens here. You see them, the poor beasts, walking with beak open and wings raised, in a lamentable and comic way.

Three years ago the last springs dried up. And the all-powerful Sun seems glorious in his immense victory.

However, there are a few trees here, a few poor trees. And there's Boghar on the right, at the summit of a dusty mountain.

On the left, crowning a hillock in a rocky fold, barely distinct from the soil, taking as it does its monotonous colouring, a large village stands up against the sky, the *ksar* of Boukhrari.

At the foot of the cone of dust which bears this vast Arab village, a few houses are hidden in the undulation of the hill; they form the *commune mixte*.

The *ksar* of Boukhrari is one of the most considerable Arab villages in Algeria. It's found just on the frontier of the South, a little beyond the Tell, in the transitional zone between the Europeanized lands and the great Desert. Its situation gives it a unique political importance, for it forms a sort of link between the coastal Arabs and the Arabs of the Sahara. It has also always been the pulse of insurrections. It's there that the watchword arrives, and from there that it sets off again. The most remote tribes send their people to Boukhrari to find out what's going on. All parts of Algeria keep an eye on this place.

Only the French administration is unconcerned with what's afoot in Boukhrari. She simply established a COMMUNE DE PLEIN EXERCICE there, [15] modelled on the French communes: administered by a mayor, an old peasant with a lazy eye, and flanked by a rural policeman. Come and go as you please. Arabs coming from anywhere can circulate, chat and intrigue as they like without being constrained by anything.

At the foot of the *ksar*, two or three hundred metres away, the *commune mixte* is governed by the civil administrator who has the most wide-stretching powers, but over a bare territory which it is almost useless to watch over. But he cannot encroach on the responsibilities of his neighbour, the mayor.

On the mountain opposite is Boghar where the senior major of the military circle resides. In his hands are the most effective means of action, but he can do nothing in the *ksar*, in the *commune de plein exercice*. Now the *ksar* is only inhabited by Arabs, but this dangerous place is respected, whilst the surroundings we carefully oversee. Harm is being dealt with in its effects, and not in its cause.

So what happens? The major and the administrator, when they listen to each other, organize a sort of secret police without the mayor's knowledge, and endeavour to be informed by clandestine means.

It's not at all surprising to see this Arab centre, considered dangerous by everyone, with greater liberty than a town in France, meanwhile it is impossible for a Frenchman, unless he is protected by a few influential persons, to enter and move about in the military territory of the advanced circles of the South.

In the *commune mixte* there is an inn. I spent the night there, it was like a night in a steam room. The air seemed burnt by the flame of the day just gone, unstirring, as though it had been solidified by the heat.

At the first glimmerings of dawn I got up. The sun appeared, relentless in its work as arsonist. In front of my open window on the already torrid and silent horizon, a small unhitched stagecoach awaited. The yellow sign read: 'Southern Mail' [Courrier du Sud]!

Southern Mail! So you could still go further south in this terrible month of August. The South! What a quick, burning word! The South! Fire! Over there, in the North, you say, in speaking of warm lands 'le Midi'. Here you say the 'South'.

I looked at this syllable, so short that it appeared surprising to me, as if I had never before read it. I was discovering in it, it seemed to me, a mysterious meaning. For the most well-known words, like oft-seen faces, have a secret significance, which you notice all of a sudden one day, you know not why.

The South! The desert, the nomads, the unexplored lands and then the negroes, a whole new world, the beginning of a universe! The south! just like that becoming energetic on the frontier of the Sahara.

In the afternoon I went to visit the *ksar*.

Boukhrari is the first village where you meet the Oulad-Naïl. You are left astonished at the appearance of these courtesans of the desert.

The populous streets are full of Arabs laid down across doorways, across the road, squatting, chatting in low voices, or sleeping. Everywhere their billowing white clothes seem to augment the unified whiteness of the houses. There are no stains, all is white; and suddenly a woman appears, standing in a doorway, with a large hairstyle apparently of Assyrian origin, upon which is mounted an enormous gold tiara.

She wears a long bright red dress. Her arms and ankles are encircled with sparkling bracelets; and her straight-lined figure is tattooed with blue stars.

Then there are more, many more, with the same monumental hairstyle: a square mountain, from which hangs on each side a great tress falling to the ear, which is then brought up behind to be lost anew in the opaque mass of hair. They always wear tiaras, some of which are extremely valuable. The bosom is drowned underneath necklaces, medallions, heavy jewellery; and two strong chains of silver fall just below the stomach where there is a big lock of the same metal, curiously engraved in openwork fashion, and the key of which hangs from the end of another chain.

Some of these girls have only thin bracelets. They are just starting out. The others, the elder ones, sometimes sport up to ten or fifteen thousand francs' worth of jewellery. I saw one whose necklace was formed of eight rows of twenty franc pieces. That's how they keep their fortune, their laboriously earned savings. The rings on their ankles are of solid silver and of a surprising weight. Indeed, as soon as they have the value of two or three hundred francs in silver coins, they give them to Mozabite [16] jewellers to melt, who then return to them these engraved rings, or symbolic locks, or chains, or large bracelets. The tiaras which crown them are obtained in the same way.

Their monumental hairstyle, a skilful and complicated tangle of twisted braids, needs nearly a day's work and an unbelievable amount of oil. As they only restyle their hair every month, they take great care not to compromise, in their loves, this high and difficult edifice of hair, which diffuses, in little time, an intolerable odour.

You have to see them in the evening when they dance in the Moorish café.

The village is quiet. White shapes lie stretched out alongside the houses. The burning night is riddled with stars; and these African stars shine with a brightness I did not know they had, like diamonds of fire, palpitating, living, acute.

Suddenly, with the turning of a street, a noise hits you, a wild and hurried music, a jerky rumble of tambourines standing out against the shrill, continuous, mind-numbing, deafening and ferocious clamour of a flute that is filled with the tireless breath of a big devil with ebony skin, the master of the establishment.

In front of the door, a heap of burnouses, a bundle of Arabs who watch without entering and who form a great glimmering under the light that comes from inside.

Inside, beneath a very low ceiling, lines of motionless and white beings are seated on benches along the white walls. And squatting on the ground, with their flamboyant finery, their sparkling jewellery, their tattooed faces, their tall, tiared hair, reminiscent of the Egyptian bas-reliefs, the Oulad-Naïl await.

We enter. Nobody moves. So, in order to sit down, and according to custom, you grab the Arabs, jostle them, fling them off their bench and they go away, impassive. Others squeeze up to make space for them.

On a platform at the back four tambourine players in ecstatic poses frenetically beat the tort skin of their instruments; and the master, the big negro, walks up and down at a majestic pace, furiously blowing into his enraged flute, without respite, without faltering for a second.

Then two Oulad-Naïl get up and go and position themselves at the edge of the space made free between the benches and they start to dance. Their dance is a gentle movement with rhythmic taps of the heel making the rings on their feet jingle. With each one of these taps the entire body bends in a kind of methodical lameness; and their hands, raised and held at eye level, are gently turned over with each twist and turning, with a vibrant flurry, a rapid shaking of the fingers. The face is turned a little, rigid, impassive and fixed, remaining amazingly motionless, the face of a sphinx, whilst the oblique gaze stays set upon the undulations of the hand, as if fascinated by this gentle movement that unceasingly cuts across the abrupt convulsion of the fingers.

They also move one towards the other. When they meet, their hands touch; they seem to quiver; they lean back at the waist, letting a large lace veil trail from their hair to their feet. They brush against each other, arched behind, like the swooning, pretty movements of amorous doves. The great veil beats like a wing. Then suddenly upright again, becoming once more impassive, they separate; each one continuing as far as the line of spectators with a slow and stuttered gliding.

Not all of them are pretty; but they are all strangely intriguing. And nothing can give a true idea of the squatting Arabs with their calm and measured bearing, in the midst of whom they pass, these girls covered in gold and flamboyant fabrics.

Sometimes they vary the gestures of their dance a little.

Formerly these prostitutes came from only one tribe, the Oulad-Naïl. They would thus amass their dowries and, after they made their fortunes, return straight home to marry. They were no less esteemed in their tribe; it was a custom. Today, although it is always said that it is the girls of Oulad-Naïl who make their distant fortunes by this means, all the tribes in fact furnish the Arab centres with courtesans.

The owner of the café where they show and offer themselves is always a negro! As soon as he sees foreigners enter, this industrialist applies to the forehead a silver five franc piece, which sticks to the skin by one knows not what procedure. And he walks across his establishment whilst ferociously playing his wild flute, stubbornly exhibiting the money with which he is tattooed, inviting the visitor to offer him the same.

Those from Oulad-Naïl who are *de grande tente* bear in their relations with their visitors all the generosity and delicacy which their origin calls for. It suffices only to admire for a second the thick rug, which serves as a bed, for the servant of the noble prostitute to carry it to her lover of a moment as soon as he gets back to his residence, the object having impressed him.

They have, like the girls in France, procurers who live off of their fatigues. Sometimes in the morning you find one of them at the bottom of a ravine, throat slit open with a knife, stripped of all her jewels. A man that she has loved has disappeared, and no one ever sees him again.

The lodgings where they receive is a narrow bedroom with earthen walls. In the oases, the ceiling is made simply of reeds bunched one on top of the other and in which armies of scorpions live. The bed is made of layers of rugs.

Rich men, Arabs or French, who want to spend a night in luxurious orgy, rent until daybreak the Moorish bath along with the servants of the place. They drink and eat in the steam room and somewhat modify the couches' traditional use as somewhere for resting.

This question of morals [*moeurs*] leads me to a very difficult subject.

Our ideas, customs, and instincts differ so completely from those that you meet in these lands, that back home you scarcely dare to speak of a vice so common over here that the Europeans are no longer even scandalized by it. You end up laughing about it, instead of being indignant. It's a very delicate matter, but one that cannot be passed over in silence when you are wanting to try and relate Arab life, to try and understand the particular character of these people.

Here at every step you encounter cases of those unnatural loves between people of the same sex that Socrates, the *friend* of Alcibiades, recommended. [17]

Often, in history, you find examples of this strange and unsavoury passion to which Caesar abandoned himself, [18] which the Romans and Greeks constantly practised, that Henri III made fashionable in France, [19] and of which many great men can be suspected. But these examples are, however, only exceptions, all the more notable because they are fairly rare. In Africa, this abnormal love has entered customs [moeurs] so deeply that the Arabs seem to consider it as natural as the other.

From where does this deviation of instinct come from? There are undoubtedly several causes. The most apparent is the scarcity of women, sequestered by the rich who have four legitimate wives and as many concubines as they can sustain. Perhaps also the ardour of the climate, which exasperates sensual desires, has blunted in the violent temperament of these men, that delicacy, decency, and cleanliness of intellect which preserves us from repugnant habits and customs.

Perhaps a kind of tradition of the morals [moeurs] of Sodom—a depraved, uncultivated heredity, the same today as it was in biblical times—is still found at home in these nomadic peoples almost incapable of civilization. [20]

Do I dare to cite a few recent examples, ever so characteristic of the power that this passion has over the Arabs?

The Turkish baths had, from its outset, amongst the boys who worked there, a little Algerian negro. After he stayed for a while in Paris, this young man came back to Africa. Now, one morning, two soldiers were found assassinated in the barracks; and the inquest quickly revealed that the murderer was none other than the former employee of the Turkish baths, [21] who, at the same time, had killed his two lovers. The intimate relations that had been established between these men were made known to him, he discovered their liaison and, jealous of both of them, strangled them.

Similar acts are very common.

Now, here is another drama.

A young Arab *de grande tente* (?) [22] was known throughout the country for his amorous habits which competed unfairly with the Oulad-Naïl.

His brothers reproached him several times, not for his habits [moeurs], but for his venality. As he wasn't changing his ways, they gave him eight days to renounce his trade. He did not take account of this warning.

On the morning of the ninth day, he was found dead, strangled in the middle of the Arab cemetery with his body naked and his head veiled. When his face was uncovered, a coin was found violently rammed into the flesh of his forehead by the kick of a heel, and on this coin, a little black stone.

After the drama, a comedy.

An officer of the spahis sought in vain for an orderly. All the soldiers that he had employed were badly dressed, careless, and impossible to retain. One morning a young Arab horseman introduced himself, he was very handsome, intelligent, and of fine bearing. The lieutenant took him on trial. He was a real find, an active, neat, taciturn boy, attentive and skilful. All went well for eight days. On the morning of the ninth day, as the lieutenant was returning from his daily walk, he noticed an old spahi in front of his door in the process of polishing his boots. He went into the hall; another spahi was sweeping. In the bedroom a third was making the bed. A fourth, in the distance, was singing in the stable, whilst the proper orderly, the young Mohammed, was lying down on a rug smoking cigarettes.

Amazed, the lieutenant called out to one of these unexpected replacements, and, pointing his comrades out to him, said: 'What the f— are you all doing here?'

The Arab immediately explained: 'My lieutenant, the native lieutenant, sent us.' (Each French lieutenant is, in effect, doubled by a native officer who is subordinate to him.)

'Ah! it's the native lieutenant. And why's that?'

'My lieutenant, he said to us: "Go to the lieutenant's place and do for me all of Mohammed's work. Mohammed is to do nothing, because he is the lieutenant's wife."'

Furthermore, this delicate attention cost the officer two months' imprisonment.

What this proves is how much this vice has entered into the customs [*moeurs*] of the Arabs, and any prisoner who falls into their hands is soon used for their pleasures. If they are numerous, the unfortunate can die following this torture of voluptuous pleasure.

When the law is called to certify a murder, it also ascertains all too often that the cadaver has been violated, after death, by the murderer.

There are still other all too common acts, so disgusting that I cannot record them here.

One evening, towards sunset, whilst coming back down from Boukhrari, I noticed three Oulad-Naïl, two in red and one in blue, standing in the middle of a crowd of men sitting in the oriental style[23] or lying down. They had the air of wild goddesses overlooking a prostrated people.

All had their eyes fixed on the fort of Boghar on the great hill opposite, the other side of the dusty valley. All were motionless, attentive as if they had been waiting for some surprise. They were all holding in their hands unlit cigarettes that they had just rolled.

Suddenly a little plume of white smoke spouted from the summit of the fortress, and at once all the cigarettes were in all the mouths, whilst a distant and muted noise made the earth tremble a little. It was the French cannon announcing to the vanquished the end of the daily abstinence.

VII

The Zar'ez

I was breakfasting one morning in the fort of Boghar at the home of the captain of the *bureau arabe*—one of the most obliging and capable officers to be found in the South, say those who should know—and there was talk of a mission about to be taken by two young lieutenants. It involved a lengthy excursion into the Boghar, Djelfa and Bou-Saada set of territories to determine the positions of water sources. A general uprising was still feared as early as the end of Ramadan and preparation was required for the march of an expeditionary column through the tribes who populated this part of the country.

There were still no precise maps of these regions, only brief topographical accounts made by those few officers who pass through from time to time—approximate indications of sources and wells in notes scrawled briskly on the pommel of the saddle, and quick sketches done by eye, without instruments of any sort.

I immediately asked for permission to join this small troop. It was granted to me with the best grace in the world.

We left two days later.

It was three o' clock in the morning when a spahi came to wake me up by knocking on the door of the poor Boukhrari inn.

When I opened up, a man presented himself wearing a red jacket embroidered with black, and baggy pleated trousers tucked in at the knee where those crimson leather stockings common to horsemen of the desert began. He was an Arab of medium build. His hooked nose had been split by a sword blow and the scar left the left nostril completely opened up. He was called Bou-Abdallah.

'Mossieu, your horse is ready.'

'Has the lieutenant arrived?' I asked.

'He's coming.'

A noise rose up in the distance, emanating from the dark, bare valley; then some shadows and silhouettes appeared and passed by. I could only make out the strange and slow bodies of three camels that were carrying canteens, our camp beds and the few things we were taking for a twenty day voyage into a wilderness that the officers themselves barely knew.

Soon after, still from the direction of the Boghar fort, the rapid galloping of a troop of horsemen resounded; and the two lieutenants who were embarking on the mission appeared with their escort, formed of another spahi and an Arab horseman named Dellis, a man *de grande tente*, from an illustrious native family.

I immediately mounted my horse and we departed.

The night continued to be uncompromising, calm, you might say motionless. We went back for a while towards the north, following the Chélif valley, then we turned right into a little valley, just as day was breaking.

In this country, dawn and dusk do not exist. You almost never see those beautiful trailing clouds that appear torn out and dabbed in crimson, so strangely mottled—as though bleeding or enflamed—that colour our Northern horizons when the sun rises and when the sun sets.

Here, at first there is a faint glimmer which increases, stretches out and invades everywhere in a few moments. All of a sudden at the crest of a mountain, or at the edge of an infinite plain, the sun appears, climbing up into the sky, lacking that flushed appearance, as if still sleeping, that the sun has on rising in our misty country.

There is something unique about dawn in the desert and that's the silence.

Back home everyone knows that the first bird call comes well before day, when the sky first begins to turn pale; then, from the neighbouring tree, another call in response; until finally there is an incessant hullabaloo of whistles, repeated ritornellos, sharp notes, and the distant and continuous crow of cocks; a clamour of wakening animals, a great mirth of voices in the foliage.

Here, nothing. The enormous sun rises up from below the earth that it has devastated, and already seems to look upon it authoritatively, as though checking that still nothing living exists there. Not an animal cry, save sometimes the whinnying of a horse; no stirring of life, except if you are camped near a well, where the long, slow, mute procession of herds come to drink.

Immediately the heat is burning. Over your flannel hood and white helmet, you wear a huge *médol*—a straw hat with an oversized brim.

Slowly we follow the valley. As far as the eye can see, everything is bare, grey-yellow, burning and superb. Sometimes, in the middle of the valley, down at the bottom where there is a remnant of stagnating water in the empty riverbeds, a few green reeds form a small, rough blot; sometimes in a fold of the mountain, two or three trees indicate a source. We were not yet in the thirsting region that we would soon have to cross.

We climbed indefinitely. Some other little valleys threw themselves into ours; and as a sign that we were approaching noon, the horizons began to lose themselves in a light heat haze, in fumes from the roasted earth that drowned the distance in tones that were barely blue, barely pink, or barely white, but nevertheless had a little of all those colours, and seemed to possess a softness, a tenderness, an infinite charm, beyond the blinding glare of the immediate landscape.

At last we arrived on the mountain peak, we were going to camp here and *caïd* El-Akhedar-ben-Yahia—whose home this was—appeared, coming towards us with a few horsemen. He was an Arab of illustrious blood, the son of bach'agha Yahia-ben-Aïssa, nicknamed the 'Bach'agha with the wooden leg'.[1]

He led us to the prepared camp, by a source, under four gigantic trees whose feet are constantly bathed in water and are the only greenery to be seen on the whole dry and stony horizon that extends about us as far as the eye can see.

Lunch is served straight away, however Ramadan prevents the *caïd* from taking part. But to make sure that we want for nothing, he sits opposite us, next to his brother, El-Haoués-ben-Yahia, *caïd* of the Oulad-Alane-Berchieh. Next I see a child approach, about twelve years of age, a little slender, but with a proud and charming grace, whom I had already noticed a few days previous in the midst of the Oulad-Naïl in the Moorish café of Boukhrari.

I had been struck by the delicate and sparkling whiteness of the clothes of this fragile little Arab, by his noble demeanour, and by the respect that everyone seemed to accord him; and, as I was astonished that, at his age, he was allowed to prowl in the midst of such courtesans, I was told: 'He's the youngest son of the bach'agha. He comes here to experience life, and to experience women!!!' As you can see, very different to our French customs [*moeurs*]!

The child recognized me too and came and gravely shook my hand. Then, as his age did not constrain him, still being young, he sat down with us and began to pick at pieces of roast mutton with his little delicate and thin fingers. And I understood that his big brothers, the two *caïds*, who must have been about forty, had been ribbing him on the journey from the *ksar*, asking him where he had got the silk tie that he was wearing around his neck, perhaps it was a gift from a lady?

That day the shade from the trees allowed us to have a siesta. I woke up as evening was falling, and I climbed a nearby hillock to have a view over the whole horizon.

The sun, close to disappearing, was tinged with red in the middle of an orange sky. And everywhere under my gaze, as far as the eye could see, from the north to the south, the east to the west, the lines of upright mountains were pink, an extravagant pink, like the colour of flamingos' feathers. It was like something from the grand finale of an enchanting opera, a remarkable and unlikely colour, something artificial, forced and against nature, but strangely admirable nevertheless.

The following day we descended once more into the plain on the other side of the mountain, a never-ending plain that took us three days to cross, even though you could distinctly see the Djebel-Gada chain which closed it opposite us.

Sometimes it was a desolate expanse of sand, or dusty earth rather, sometimes a sea of esparto tufts stuck randomly into the soil meaning our horses could only proceed in zig-zags.

The African plains are remarkable.

They appear flat and bare like a parquet floor, but in actual fact there are constant undulations, like a sea after a storm which from afar seems totally calm because the surface is smooth, but which is stirred by long quiet swells. The slopes of these waves of earth are imperceptible; never do you lose sight of the mountains on the horizon, but in a parallel undulation, two kilometres from you, an army could be hiding and you would not see it.

It was this that made the pursuit of Bou-Amama on the hauts plateaux of the Sud-Oranais esparto farmers so difficult.

Each morning from daybreak we start walking across these interminable and desolate expanses; each evening we notice a few men on horseback, draped in white, coming to lead us towards a patched up tent under which rugs are spread out. Every day we eat the same things, chat a bit, then sleep, or dream.

And if you knew how far away you were, how far away from the world, from life, from everything, under this low little tent through the holes of which you can see the stars, and through its raised sides, the immense land of dry sand!

The land out there is monotonous, always the same, always charred and dead; but out there, however, you desire nothing, you aspire to nothing. This calm landscape, desolate and streaming with light is enough for the eye, is enough for the mind, and satisfies the senses and the dreams because it is complete, *absolute*, and you couldn't conceive of it any other way. The all too rare greenery that is found there jars like something false, offensive and harsh.

Every day at the same times, it's the same spectacle: fire eating a world; and, as soon as the sun has set, the moon, in her turn, rises over the infinite solitude. But, each day, little by little, the silent desert invades you, penetrating your mind as the harsh light chars your skin; and you'd like to become a nomad there in the way that these men change lands without ever changing their fatherland, in the midst of these interminable spaces always so similar.

Each day the officer on tour sends ahead a native horseman to warn the *caïd* at whose place they will eat and sleep the following day, so that he can levy from his tribe food for the men and animals. This custom which is the equivalent of billeting lodgings with the inhabitants of towns in France has become extremely burdensome for the tribes through the way in which it is practised.

Who says Arab, says thief, without exception. This is what happens. The *caïd* addresses a head of a faction and claims these dues from his men.

To exempt himself from this duty, this corvée, the head of the faction pays instead. The *caïd* pockets the money and applies to another who often also exonerates himself in the same way. But in the end it is necessary that someone carries out the levy.

If the *caïd* has an enemy, the load falls upon him, and he proceeds in the same manner with common Arabs as the *caïd* has just done with the sheikhs.

And so this is how a duty which shouldn't cost each tribe more than twenty or thirty francs, invariably ends up costing four or five hundred francs.

And, for countless reasons too lengthy to go into here, it's impossible to change that.

As soon as you approach one of these campsites, you see in the distance a group of horsemen coming towards you. One of them walking alone at the front. They go at walking pace, or at a trot. Then all of a sudden they launch into a gallop, a furious gallop that our Northern beasts couldn't sustain for more than two minutes. It's the gallop of racehorses that resemble, as they go past, an express train. But the Arab remains almost upright in his saddle, with his white clothes billowing. And in one movement he brings the animal to a halt, the horse flexing its legs, the rider jumping on to the ground with a single bound and advancing respectfully towards the officer, whose hand he then kisses.

Whatever the title of the Arab, whatever his origin, power and fortune, he nearly always kisses the hand of the officers that he meets.

Then the *caïd* gets back into his saddle and directs the travellers towards the tent that he has prepared for them. It's generally imagined that Arab tents are white, sparkling under the sun. On the contrary, they are of a dirty brown with yellow stripes. Their very thick fabric, of camel or goat skin, seems coarse. The tent is extremely low (one can just about stand up in them) and very wide. Stakes support it in a fairly irregular way, and all the sides are raised to allow the air to circulate freely within.

In spite of this precaution, the heat in these canvas dwellings is crushing during the day; but the nights spent in them are sweet, and you sleep marvellously on thick, magnificent rugs from Djebel-Amour, in spite of them being populated with insects.

The rugs constitute the only luxury of wealthy Arabs. They pile them up one on top of the other in a heap, and they respect them greatly, for each man takes off his shoes before walking on them, as is done at the door of mosques.

As soon as his guests are seated, or rather stretched out on the ground, the *caïd* orders coffee to be brought. This coffee is exquisite. The recipe however is simple. They crush it instead of grinding it, and mix it with a sizeable quantity of ambergris, then they boil it in water.

There is nothing so funny as Arab crockery. When a wealthy *caïd* receives you, his tent is decorated with invaluable hangings, admirable cushions and marvellous rugs; then you see arriving an old sheet metal tray bearing four chipped, cracked, hideous cups, which look like they've been bought from some outdoor market stall on a Paris street. They are in all their shapes and sizes—English

The Zar'ez

porcelain, Japanese imitations, common Creil [2]—the ugliest and crudest earthenware that is made from all four corners of the globe.

The coffee is brought in a teapot, or in an old private's mess tin, or in a deformed, dented lead coffee pot that looks in a bad state and is beyond description.

A strange, childish people who have remained primitive since the birth of man. They go across the earth without attaching themselves to it, without settling on it. For houses they only have linen stretched over sticks, they don't possess any of those objects that for us life would seem impossible without. No beds, no sheets, no tables, no seats, none of those little indispensable things that make life more comfortable. No furniture, for there's nothing to put away, no industry, no art, no knowledge of anything. They can barely sew the goatskins for carrying water, and in all situations they employ such crude procedures that you're left stupefied.

They cannot even repair a tent that has been ripped by the wind; and the holes in this brownish fabric are numerous, the rain getting through at will. They seem to be neither attached to the soil nor life, these vagabond horsemen who place a single stone on the place where their dead sleep, any old rock collected from the neighbouring mountain. Their cemeteries resemble fields where at some time or another a European house might have tumbled down.

The negroes have huts, the Lapps have holes, the Eskimos have igloos, the wildest of the wild have dwellings dug into the soil or fixed above it; they hold the earth as their mother. The Arabs pass by, always wandering, without attachments, without tenderness for this earth that we possess, that we render fertile, that we love with the very fibres of our human heart; they pass by, galloping on their horses, unfitted to all our work, indifferent to our concerns, as if they were always going somewhere where they will never arrive.

Their customs have stayed rudimentary. Our civilization slips past without touching them.

They drink from the same goatskin; but they present water to strangers in an unlikely collection of receptacles. Anything they can find, from an iron saucepan to a bashed-in can. If they were to seize in some raid or another one of our Parisian top hats, they would surely preserve it in order to offer a drink from it to the first general that came across the tribe.

Their cooking is formed solely of four or five dishes. The order of these dishes doesn't vary.

Presented first off is the sheep roasted in the open air. A man carries the whole thing on his shoulder on the end of a pole which serves as a skewer; and the silhouette of the skinned animal, perched up in the air, makes you think of some kind of medieval execution. Thus held by an austere character cloaked in white, it presents a sinister and burlesque profile against the red evening sky.

This sheep is deposited in a flat basket of braided esparto, in the middle of the diners who are seated cross-legged in a circle. The fork is unknown; you pick with your fingers or with a small indigenous horn-handled knife. The browned skin, crispy and glazed by the fire, is taken for the finest of things. You tear it in long strips and crunch it whilst drinking muddy water, or camel's milk cut fifty-fifty with water, or some bitter milk that has fermented in a goatskin, from which it gets an extremely musky flavour. The Arabs call this mediocre drink 'leben'.[3]

After the *entrée*, a type of vermicelli mash appears, sometimes in a bowl, sometimes in a basin, sometimes in a cooking pot. At the bottom of this soup is yellowish juice where pimento fights with red pepper in a mixture of dried apricots and dates crushed together.

I do not recommend this broth to gourmands.

When you are received by an especially grand *caïd*, you are next served with the *hamis*; this food is remarkable. I will perhaps be of service to some people in giving the recipe.

It is prepared either with chicken or with mutton. After having cut the meat into little pieces you brown it with butter in a frying pan.

Next you make a light broth by watering the meat with some hot water (I believe that it would be better to use a weak broth prepared in advance). You add great quantities of red pepper, a soupçon of pimento, some ordinary pepper, salt, some onions, some dates and dried apricots, and you cook until the dates and apricots crumble up naturally, then you pour this juice on to the meat. It's exquisite.

The meal invariably finishes with couscous or *kouskoussou*, the national dish. The Arabs prepare the couscous by rolling the flour in their hands in a way that forms little grains similar to hunting shot. These granules are cooked in a particular way and watered with a special broth. I will stay silent on these recipes in case anyone accuses me of speaking only about cuisine.

Sometimes little rolled and flaky honey cakes are served, which are extremely good.

The Zar'ez

Each time you take a drink, the hosting *caïd* says to you: *Saa!* (good health!). You must reply: *Allah y selmeck!* which is the equivalent of our 'God bless you!' These phrases are repeated ten times over during each meal.

Every evening towards four o' clock we settle under a new tent; sometimes at the foot of a mountain, sometimes in the middle of an unbounded plain.

As news of our arrival spreads amongst the tribe, little white dots are seen in the distance all around, approaching from the sterile countryside or the hilltops. They are the Arabs coming to gaze upon the officer and address their complaints to him. Most of them are on horse, some on foot; a large number are mounted on little donkeys. They ride pillion astride the rump, by the tail of the toddling animals, and their long bare feet trail in the earth on either side.

As soon as they descend their mounts they come and crouch around the tent; and they stay there, motionless, eyes fixed, waiting. Finally the *caïd* signals and the plaintiffs present themselves.

All officers on duty administer justice in a sovereign manner.

They bring unlikely complaints, for no people are so fond of lawsuits, quarrelling, litigation and vengeance as the Arab people. As for knowing the truth, as for giving a fair trial, it is totally useless to think of anything like that. Each party brings forth a fantastic number of false witnesses who swear on the bones of their fathers and mothers, and affirm under oath the most shameless lies.

Here are a few examples:

A *cadi*[4] (the venality of these Muslim magistrates is proverbial and by no means surpassed) calls up an Arab and addresses this proposal to him: 'You will give me twenty-five douros[5] and bring me seven witnesses who will set it down in writing in front of me that X owes you seventy-five douros. I will make him give it back to you.'

The man brings forth his witnesses who set down and sign their statements. Then the cadi calls forth X and says to him: 'You will give me fifty douros and bring me nine witnesses who will state that B (the first Arab) owes you one hundred and twenty-five douros. I will make him give it back to you.' The second Arab brings forth his witnesses.

And so the cadi calls the first in front of him, backed up by the depositions of seven witnesses, and makes the second pay him the seventy-five douros. But, in his turn, the second complains, and, with the testimonies of his nine witnesses, the cadi makes the first [Arab] pay him one hundred and twenty-five douros.

For his part the magistrate gets seventy-five douros (375 fr.), levied from his two victims.

This is authenticated fact.

Nevertheless, the Arab almost never addresses himself to the French Justice of the Peace, because he can't corrupt him, whilst the cadi will do what you want for money.

He [the Arab] feels an insurmountable repugnance for the fussy and interfering methods of our justice system. Any written procedure terrifies him, because he possesses to the utmost a superstitious fear of paper, on which you can put the name of God, or trace the characters of evil spells. [6]

At the start of French domination, when the Muslims found in their path any old scrap of paper, they would raise it piously to their lips and bury it in the ground or stuff it into a hole in a wall or tree. This habit led to so many disagreeable surprises that the Mohammedans soon cured themselves of it.

Another example of Arab treachery.

In a tribe from near Boghar, a murder was committed. An Arab was suspected, but there was a lack of evidence. There was in this tribe a poor man, newly arrived from a neighbouring tribe, who had set up there to safeguard his pecuniary interests. A witness accused him of the murder. Another witness followed the first, then another. Ninety came forward with the most precise statements. The stranger was condemned to death and executed. The innocence of the decapitated man was known from the off. The Arabs had simply wanted to do away with a stranger that bothered them, and prevent a man from their tribe being *compromised*!

The lawsuits can last for years without a glimmer of truth appearing in the statements of false witnesses. And so recourse has been made to a very simple means: The two contesting families along with all their witnesses are imprisoned. They are released after a few months; and generally they keep the peace for about a year. Then they begin again.

There was in the tribe of the Oulad-Alane, whom we ran across, a trial which had gone on for three years without any sign of resolution. The two plaintiffs were locked up, from time to time, for a little spell, and then they began again.

They spend the rest of their lives stealing from each other, cheating each other and shooting each other. But as far as possible they conceal from us all the cases where guns have been involved.

The Zar'ez

Amongst the Oulad-Mokhtar, a man of big build asks to be admitted to the French hospital.

The officer questions him about his illness. The Arab pulls aside his clothing and we are confronted with a horrible wound about where the liver is, already very old and purulent. Having asked the man to turn around, we see another hole in the centre of his back, opposite the first, and about the size of a child's head. Around where the wound has been pressed, fragments of bone have protruded. This man has obviously been shot; and the charge has entered under the chest and exited through the back, breaking two or three ribs. But he emphatically denies this, swears and protests that 'it's the work of God'.

Besides in this dry country wounds don't present a grave danger. Fermentations and decay produced by the hatching of microbes do not exist, these animalcules only live in damp climates.[7] If you are not killed by the shot and if the vital organs are not destroyed, the wounds always heal.

The following day we arrived at the home of the *caïd* Abd-el-Kader-bel-Hout, a parvenu. The tribe that he governs over wisely is less turbulent and less litigious than the others. Perhaps we have to look for another reason for this relative tranquillity.

The region only having sources on the no longer inhabited southern slope of Djebel-Gada, water is naturally only supplied by wells common to the whole tribe. Therefore no *diverting of the water from its course* can occur, which is the principal cause of all quarrels and hatred in the south.

Here, once again, a man presented himself, soliciting admission to the French hospital. When he was asked what illness he had, he lifted up his *gandoura*[8] and showed his legs. They were marbled with blue bruises, flabby, limp and soft like an overripe fruit, with flesh so soft that the finger pressed into it like dough, and the mark of this impression was left behind for a long time. This poor devil exhibited all the symptoms of a terrible syphilis. When he was asked how this infirmity had come about, he raised his hand and swore on the memory of his ancestors that 'it was the work of God'.

In truth the God of the Arabs carries out some very strange works.

Since all complaints had been heard, we tried to get a little sleep in the awful heat of the tent.

Then evening comes; we dine. A deep calm falls on the charred earth. The dogs of the *douars* begin to howl in the distance, and the jackals answer them.

We stretch out on rugs beneath a sky riddled with stars, limpid in their scintillating clarity; and we chat for a long time, a very long time. Memories come back, pleasant, precise and easy to tell under these mild nights so full of stars.

All around the officer's tent, Arabs are spread out on the ground; and the horses stay standing in a line, with their front legs fettered, a man on guard near each one of them.

They mustn't go to bed; and they always remain standing, these horses; for a chief's mount cannot be tired. Sometimes they try to lie down, then an Arab rushes over and forces them to get back up again.

But the night moves on. We stretch out on thick woollen rugs and sometimes on sudden awakenings we notice, all over the bare earth that surrounds us, white beings stretched out, sleeping, like cadavers under shrouds.

One day, after a ten hour hike in the burning dust, when we had just arrived at a camp situated close by to a well of muddy and brackish water (which nevertheless seemed exquisite to us), the lieutenant suddenly grabbed me just as I was going to rest in the tent and, pointing at the distant horizon to the south, said to me: 'Do you see anything over there?'

After having looked for a bit, I replied: 'Yes, a very small grey cloud.'

And the lieutenant smiled: 'Ah good! Sit down there and continue to watch this cloud.'

Surprised, I asked why. My companion resumed: 'If I'm not mistaken, a sandstorm is on its way to us.'

It was about four o' clock and the temperature was still forty-eight degrees in the tent. The air seemed to be drowsing under the oblique and unbearable flames of the sun. No breath, no noise, save the chomping jaws of our fettered horses who were eating barley, and the indistinct whisperings of some Arabs a hundred paces away who were preparing our meal.

There was, however, another heat surrounding us, more concentrated, more suffocating than that from the sky, rather like the heat which oppresses you when you find yourself in the neighbourhood of a massive fire. It wasn't like the abrupt, repeated gusts of burning wind and caresses of fire that announce and precede the sirocco, but instead a mysterious heating up of every atom of every thing in existence.

The Zar'ez

I was watching the cloud grow rapidly bigger, in the same way as all clouds do. It was now a dirty brown and rising very high into space. Then it broadened out, as do our storms in the north. In truth, it didn't seem anything special to me.

But soon it had blocked out the whole of the south. Its base was of an opaque black, its copper-coloured summit almost transparent.

A big commotion behind me made me turn around. The Arabs had closed our tent, weighing down the sides with heavy stones. Everyone was running, calling out, flinging themselves about in the bewildered manner you see in a camp at the time of an attack.

It seemed to me that the day suddenly dwindled; I raised my eyes towards the sun. It was covered in a yellow veil and seemed to be no more than a rapidly disappearing, pale, round stain.

Next I saw an astonishing spectacle. The whole of the southern horizon had disappeared, and a nebulous mass that rose all the way to the zenith was coming towards us, eating up objects, reducing with every second the field of vision, drowning everything.

Instinctively I moved back towards the tent. It was time. The hurricane, like a boundless yellow wall, hit us. This wall arrived with the rapidity of a train going at full speed; and suddenly it enveloped us in a furious whirlwind of sand and wind, in a burning, rumbling, blinding and suffocating storm of impalpable earth.

Our tent, upheld by enormous stones, was shaken like a sail, but resisted. That of our spahis, less secure, fluttered for a few seconds, the canvas being greatly rippled; then all of a sudden it was torn up from the ground, flew away and had soon disappeared into the night of shifting dust which surrounded us.

In this sandy darkness you couldn't see more than ten paces in front of you. You breathed in sand, drunk sand and ate sand. Your eyes were filled by it, your hair was powdered in it; it slipped down our necks, up our sleeves and into our boots.

This lasted all night. A burning thirst tortured us. But the water, the milk, the coffee, all were full of sand which grated in our teeth. The roast mutton was powdered in it; the couscous seemed to be made entirely of finely grained gravel; the flour of the bread was no more than finely crushed stone.

A big scorpion came to see us. This weather, which is pleasing to these beasts, makes them all come out of their holes. The dogs of the neighbouring *douar* were not howling this night.

Then, in the morning, it was all over; and the great murdering tyrant of Africa, the superb sun, rose over the clear horizon.

We left a little late, the flooding of sand having disturbed our sleep.

The Djebel-Gada chain, which we had to cross, rose up in front of us. A pass opened up on the right; we followed the mountains to this passage, where we undertook the crossing. We found once more esparto, horrible esparto. Then all of a sudden I thought I had discovered the faded out marks of a road, the ruts of wheels. I stopped, surprised. How strange, a road here? I was given the explanation. A former *caïd* of this tribe, having been intoxicated by the example of the Europeans living in Algiers, wanted to give himself the luxury of a coach in the desert. But in order to have a coach, he needed to have roads, and so for many months this ingenious potentate, and all his subjects, the Arabs, were kept busy with work on a great roadway system. These poor wretches, without pickaxes, shovels and tools, more often than not digging up embankments with their bare hands, nevertheless somehow managed to level out several kilometres of roadway. That was sufficient for their master, who thus offered trips across the Sahara in a stupefying carriage and horses, in the company of native beauties that had been sent for from Djelfa by his favourite, a young sixteen-year-old Arab.

This threadbare, corroded, stripped country has to be seen; you have to know the Arab with his imperturbable gravity in order to understand the infinite comedy of this vulture-headed libertine, this dandy of the desert promenading barefoot tarts in a crude wooden cart with uneven wheels driven from the back by his. . . mignon. This tropical elegance, this Saharan debauchery, this sally at chic in mid-Africa, seemed to me an unforgettable drollery.

Our troop was numerous that morning. Besides the *caïd* and his son, we were accompanied by two native horsemen and an old, lean man who had a sharp-pointed beard and a hooked nose, and had the physiognomy of a rat, with obsequious manners, all kow-towing and fawning. He too was a former *caïd* of the tribe, dismissed for misappropriating funds. He was to serve us as guide the following day, the road that we were going to follow being little frequented by the Arabs themselves.

Little by little we arrived at the top of the pass. A sheer peak barred the view, but as soon as we had circumvented it, I was struck by, undoubtedly, the most violent of surprises that this trip held in store for me.

The Zar'ez

A vast plain stretched out in front of us, then a lake, an immense lake—dazzling in the sun, blinding—the other side of which I couldn't see, lost in the horizon to the left, and the western edge of which was located nearly opposite me. A lake in this region, in the middle of the Sahara? A lake that nobody had told me about, that no traveller had pointed out? Was I mad?

I turned towards the lieutenant.

'What is that lake?' I asked him.

He began to laugh and replied:

'That's not water, that's salt. Everyone makes that mistake, so perfect is the illusion. This *Sebkra*,[9] which they call here Zar'ez (the Zar'ez-Chergui), is about fifty to sixty kilometres long and twenty, thirty or forty kilometres wide, from place to place. The figures are, as you might well understand, approximate, this land having only ever been rarely and rapidly crossed, just as it will be by us today. These lakes of salt (there are two, the other found further west) give their name to this whole region, which is called the Zar'ez. From Bou-Saada onwards the plain is called the Hodna, so baptized after the salt lake of Msila.'

I looked with wondrous amazement at the huge blanket of salt sparkling under the raging sun of these regions. The whole surface, flat and crystallized, glimmered like an incommensurable mirror, like a sheet of steel; the glare from this strange lake unbearable upon burning eyes, although it was still twenty kilometres from us, which I found hard to believe, so close did it appear to me.

We finished our descent down the other side of the Djebel-Gada, and we approached an abandoned fortified post, called the poste de la Fontaine (Bordj-el-Hammam), where we were to camp, this stage of the journey being, extraordinarily, very short.

The crenellated building was built at the start of the conquest in order to be able to occupy this lost region in case of insurrection and to leave a troop there with a little bit of security. Today it is derelict. The enclosing wall is however still in a fairly good state, and a few rooms have been kept inhabitable.

Like the preceding days, until evening we saw processions of Arabs who were coming to explain to 'the officer' infinitely muddled affairs or imaginary grievances with the sole intention of speaking to a French authority.

A madwoman, coming from who knows where, living one knows not how in these desolate wildernesses, prowled ceaselessly about us. As soon as we left we found her once more, squatting in bizarre postures, almost naked, hideous.

Poeticizing travellers have spoken much about the respect the Arabs have for the mad. But this is how they respect them: in their families...they kill them! Several *caïds*, pressed with questions, have admitted it to us. It's true, some of these poor idiots happen upon holiness through their cretinism. But these cases aren't exclusively limited to Africa. The family, in general, rids itself of these demented people. The tribes remain to us a closed world, and thanks to the system of the great native chiefs, more often than not, we won't even have a suspicion of these disappearances.

As I had not walked far during the day, I wrote for part of the night. Towards eleven o' clock, it being very hot, I went out to lay down a rug in front of the door and sleep beneath the sky.

The full moon filled the heavens with a glossy light which seemed to leave a glazed trail behind it. The mountains, already yellow from the sun, the yellow sands, the yellow horizon, seemed still yellower, caressed by the saffron glimmer of the stars.

Out there in front of me the Zar'ez, the huge lake of congealed salt, seemed incandescent. You might say that a fantastic phosphorescence was released from it, floating above it, a luminous mist of fairyhood, something supernatural, and oh so pleasant, capturing both the gaze and the thoughts, so much so that I stayed looking at it for over an hour, unable to find the resolve to close my eyes. And everywhere about me, also sparkling under the moon's caress, the burnouses of sleeping Arabs, resembling enormous flakes of snow.

We left as the sun was rising.

The plain leading towards the *Sebkra* was weakly inclined and sown with thin, russet esparto. The old rat-faced Arab took the lead, and we followed him at a rapid pace. The closer we got, the greater was the illusion of water. How could it not be a lake, a giant lake? Its breadth, on our left, took up all of the space between the two mountains, a distance of thirty to forty kilometres. We walked towards its right extremity to cross it at its narrowest point.

But on the other side of the Zar'ez I noticed a sort of hill or rather a yellow-gold strip which seemed separate from the mountain. On our left this line followed the white line of salt as far as the horizon; and, on our right, where a boundless and bare plain stretched out between the two mountains, I could make out as far

The Zar'ez

as the eye could see this same yellow trail. The lieutenant said to me, 'Those are the dunes. This bank of sand is over two hundred kilometres long, and of a very variable width. We will cross them tomorrow.'

The soil was becoming quite peculiar, covered by a crust of saltpetre which was punctured by the feet of the horses. Grasses showed themselves, rushes; it felt as though, perhaps, the water level had risen to just above the ground. This plain, which was enclosed by mountains, soaked up four rivers (periodic rivers) and received all the furious downpours of winter, and it would be an immense marsh if the terrible sun didn't dry out the surface of it. Sometimes, in the hollows, puddles of brackish water appeared; and snipes flew away in front of us in that rapid arc which is peculiar to them.

Then all of a sudden we were at the edge of the *Sebkra*; and we embarked across this dried up ocean.

Everything in front of us was white, the silvery white of snow, vaporous and shimmering. Even when advancing upon this crystallized surface, powdered with a dust of salt akin to a fine snow, and which sometimes sank a little under the tread of the animals, like a sludge, you retained the peculiar impression that what you beheld in front of your eyes was a sheet of water. To the trained eye there was only one thing which indicated that this was not a liquid expanse: the horizon. Ordinarily the line which separates the water from the sky remains perceptible, the one being always more or less dark than the other. Sometimes, admittedly, everything seems to merge; the sea taking on the same shade as the sky, as waves dissolve into large blue clouds, losing themselves in the paling azure of the infinite void. But it only suffices to look attentively for a few seconds to be able to distinguish the separation, faint and shrouded though it may be. Here one sees nothing. The horizon is totally veiled in a white mist, a sort of milky vapour, of indescribable softness; sometimes you are looking up into space for the earthly limit, and sometimes you believe you see it way too low down, in the middle of the salty plain upon which float these strange and creamy mists.

All the while we were overlooking the Zar'ez, we had a clear perception of distances and forms; now we were upon it any certainty of view disappeared; we found ourselves surrounded by the phantasmagorias of mirage.

Sometimes we believed we could make out the horizon a phenomenal distance away; and we suddenly noticed in the middle of this solidified lake, which a few moments ago seemed plain, empty and flat like a mirror, some enormous and fantastic boulders, huge reeds, islands with sheer banks. Then, as we advanced, these strange visions abruptly disappeared, as though swallowed up by some piece of stage-show trickery; and, in the place of the massive blocks of rock, we find a few little stones. The giant reeds, on closer inspection, are nothing more than dried blades of grass, no taller than a finger, made immeasurably big by a curious optical effect; the sheer banks turn out to be slight bulges in the saline crust, and the horizon which we supposed to be thirty kilometres away has been closed to a hundred metres from us by this tremulous veil of mist that the furious desert sun makes rise from the burning layer of salt.

That all lasted about an hour, then we reached the other shore.

It was initially a small furrowed plain, covered with a dry clay crust, mixed with saltpetre.

We climbed an imperceptible slope, grasses appeared, then species of rushes, then a little blue flower resembling the rustic forget-me-not, mounted on a long thin stalk like a wire, and so fragrant that its perfume covered the whole area. This exquisite, fresh scent gave me the impression of a bath; inhaling it for a while the chest seems to expand to drink in this delicious breath.

We finally saw a row of poplars, a veritable wood of reeds; some other trees, then we pitched our tents on the edge of the sand dunes, whose uneven undulations, as high as eight or ten metres, rose up like breaking waves.

The heat was becoming ferocious, no doubt doubled by the reflection from the *Sebkra*. The tents, like real steam rooms, were uninhabitable; and as soon as we dismounted from our horses, we left to search for the shade of the trees. First of all we had to cross a forest of reeds. I was walking in front and suddenly I began to dance, uttering cries of joy. I had just spotted some vines, some apricot trees, fig trees, and pomegranate trees all covered with fruits—a whole succession of once prosperous gardens, now invaded by the sands, which belonged to the agha of Djelfa. No roast mutton for lunch! What happiness! No couscous! What delirium! Grapes! figs! apricots! None of it was particularly ripe. But it didn't matter, this was a veritable orgy, a true feast, although we were to feel a little sick from it afterwards. The water, for example, left a lot to be desired, muddy and full of larvae. We hardly drunk any of it.

We each disappeared into the reeds and fell asleep. A cold sensation made me jump up wide awake; an enormous frog had just spat a jet of water into my face.

The Zar'ez

In this region you need to be on your guard, and it's not always wise to sleep underneath the rare verdure, especially where there are neighbouring sand dunes, for this is where the *léfaa* is found in profusion. Also known as the horny viper or *vipère céraste*, it has a deadly, vicious bite. [10] The death throes usually don't last more than an hour. This snake is very slow-moving and only becomes dangerous if you step on it unwittingly, or if you go to sleep in its vicinity. When you encounter them on the road you can even, with practice and caution, pick them up by grabbing them just behind the ears.

I didn't attempt this exercise.

This awful little creature also lives in the esparto, under rocks, any place where it can find cover. When you go to sleep for the first time al fresco, thoughts of this snake preoccupy you; soon you think about them no more. As for scorpions, we detested them. What's more, they are as common over there as spiders are back home. When we noticed one near our camp, we'd surround it in a circle of dried grass which we'd set fire to. The beast, thrown into a panic and sensing all was lost, would raise its tail, bringing it back over its head, where it would then kill itself by stinging itself. At least I was told that it killed itself, for I always saw it die in the flames.

Here is how I came to see this viper [the *léfaa*] for the first time.

One afternoon as we were crossing a vast esparto plain, my horse several times exhibited sure signs of uneasiness. It lowered its head, snorted, stopped, seeming suspicious of each tuft. I am, I have to admit, a very bad horseman, and these abrupt haltings, in addition to throwing my balance into great disarray, rammed the huge nose of my Arab saddle sharply into my stomach. The lieutenant, my companion, laughed wholeheartedly. Suddenly my animal reared up and began to look at something on the ground that I couldn't see, stubbornly refusing to advance. Foreseeing an accident, I preferred to get down and look for the cause of this fright. There was in front of me a meagre tuft of esparto. I beat it randomly with a stick; suddenly a small serpent fled, disappearing into the neighbouring plant.

It was a *léfaa*.

On the evening of the same day, in a bare, rocky plain, my horse shied again. I leapt down, persuaded that I would find another *léfaa*. But I saw nothing. Then on disturbing a stone, a long-legged spider, blonde like the sand, svelte and unusually quick, fled and disappeared under a rock before I could reach it. A spahi who had joined me called it 'a scorpion of the wind', a colourful term to express its speed. It was, I believe, a tarantula.

Another night, as I was sleeping, something icy touched my face. I jumped up, frightened; but the sand, the tent, everything was lost in shadow, I could only make out the big white blots of the Arabs sleeping around us. Had I been bitten by a *léfaa* that was passing close to my face? Very anxious, I lit our lantern; I lowered my eyes, foot raised, ready to strike, and I saw a monstrous toad, one of those fantastic white toads you find in the desert, who was looking at me with his stomach puffed out and his feet placed wide apart. The hideous beast had undoubtedly found me across his habitual path and had run into my face.

For vengeance I made him smoke a cigarette. And he died because of it. This is how you do it. You force open the narrow mouth; and you place in it a cigarette paper rolled full of tobacco; and you light the other end. The suffocating animal blows with all his vigour to dislodge this instrument of torture, then, whether he likes it or not, he is forced to inhale. And so he blows anew, inflated, exhaling and comical; and he must smoke on right until the end, at least if you don't have any pity on him. They generally die suffocated and swollen up like a balloon.

Strangers are often made to witness a kind of Saharan sport, the fight between a *léfaa* and an *ouran*.[11]

Who has not come across those poor little lizards with their tails cut off, running along old walls in the Midi? You start to wonder what the story behind these absent tails is. Then one day, as you are reading in the shade of a hedge, you all of a sudden see a snake [*couleuvre*] slithering out of a crevice and advancing upon the innocent and gentle creature basking on a stone. The lizard flees, but, quicker, the snake seizes it by the tail, by the long restless tail, and half of this member stays behind between the pointed teeth of the enemy, whilst the mutilated animal disappears into a hole.

Oh well! the *ouran*, which is none other than the land crocodile that Herodotus speaks of,[12] a sort of fat Saharan lizard, avenges his race on the terrible *léfaa*.

The battle between these animals is of great interest. It generally takes place in an old box. You put the lizard in it which begins to run around with great speed, looking to escape; but as soon as the little bag containing the viper is emptied into the box, it freezes. Its rapidly flickering eye is the only thing that moves. Then he takes a few quick sliding steps, to get closer to the enemy, and he waits. The *léfaa*, on her part, considers the lizard, senses danger and prepares itself for battle; the *léfaa* recoils and throws itself upon the lizard. But the lizard is already gone, like a shooting arrow, hardly visible in its course. He attacks in his turn, coming back with a strike of surprising rapidity. The *léfaa* turns itself over and stretches her little open mouth towards the lizard, ready to bite him with her lethal bite. But brushing against the snake, he's passed, out of reach, on the other side of the crate, regarding her once more.

And that lasts a quarter of an hour, twenty minutes, sometimes more. The *léfaa*, exasperated, gets angry, and slides towards the *ouran* which flees continually, more supple than it looks, coming back, turning, stopping, setting off again, exhausting and disorientating his formidable opponent. Then suddenly, having chosen the moment, he flies at it so quickly that the next thing you see is the contorted viper, strangled by the strong triangular jaws of the lizard, who has seized it by the neck, just behind the ears, at the same spot where the Arabs take hold of it.

Whilst watching these little creatures fight at the bottom of an old box, you are reminded of Spanish bull fights in majestic circuses. It would be more terrible, however, to disturb these slight combatants than it would be to face the bellowing anger of the great beast armed with pointed horns.

In the Sahara you often encounter a serpent that is frightful to see,[13] often over a metre in length, but no fatter than your little finger. Around Bou-Saada this inoffensive snake inspires among the Arabs a superstitious terror. They claim that it can pierce even the hardest of bodies like a bullet, that nothing can stop its momentum once it has seen a shiny object. An Arab told me that his brother had been run through by one of these beasts which in the same blow had wrung off the stirrups. It's obvious that this man had simply been shot at the same time as he saw the snake.

Around Laghouat the serpent, on the contrary, instils no fear whatsoever and children pick them up in their hands.

Thinking about all these formidable inhabitants of the desert prevented me from getting any sleep underneath the reeds of Raïane Chergui. Any rustling near my ears made me get up brusquely.

The day dwindled, I woke up my companions so that we could go and walk in the dunes and try and find a *léfaa* or a sand fish.

To the Sun

The animal that is known as the sand fish, and that the Arabs call *dwb* (pronounced *dob*) [14] is another sort of big lizard which lives in the sand dunes, where it digs its hole, and whose meat is rather good, so they say. We had often followed its tracks without succeeding in finding one. In the sand you also encounter a very little insect with very intriguing habits [*moeurs*]: the ant lion. It makes a crater a little broader than a ten sous piece, dug out in proportion, and it installs itself at the bottom, waiting in ambush. As soon as any creature, a spider, a larva or something else slips down on to the steep sides of its den, the ant lion, using grains of sand as ammunition, then launches round after round of gunfire at it, stunning it, blinding it, the force tumbling its prey down to the bottom of the slope! Then he lays hold of it and eats it.

The ant lion was, on that day, our greatest distraction. The evening brought the return of roast mutton, couscous, and bitter milk. When meal times approached I often thought about the Café Anglais. [15]

Then we went to bed on rugs in front of the tents, the heat not allowing us to stay inside. And we had, one in front of us, one behind, two of the strangest neighbours: the surging sand like an agitated sea, and the level salt, like a calm sea.

The following day we crossed the dunes. It was like an Ocean turned to dust in the middle of a hurricane; a silent storm of enormous motionless waves of yellow sand. These waves were as big as hills, uneven, varying and rising up like unleashed swells, yet bigger and streaked like moiré. On this furious sea, mute and without movement, the devouring sun of the south poured its implacable and direct flames.

We had to climb these waves of golden ash, tumbling down the other side, climbing once more, ceaselessly climbing without respite, without shade. The horses groan, sink up to their knees and slide as they tear down the other sides of these astonishing hills.

We no longer speak, overwhelmed by the heat and a thirst as desiccated as this burning desert.

It is said that sometimes in these valleys of sand you are surprised by an incomprehensible phenomenon which the Arabs consider a sure sign of death.

Somewhere nearby, from an indeterminable direction, a drum beats, the mysterious drum of the dunes. It beats distinctly, sometimes more vibrant, sometimes weaker, stopping, then reprising its fantastic rumble.

The Zar'ez

No one knows, it seems, what the cause of this astonishing noise is. It's generally attributed to an echo—augmented, multiplied and immeasurably swollen by the undulations of the dunes—of a hail of grains of sand carried up by the wind and thrown on to tufts of dry grass, for it has been noted that the phenomenon is always produced in places near where there are little plants that have been burnt up by the sun, hardened like parchment.

This drumbeat would thus only be a kind of mirage of sound.

As soon as we left the dunes we noticed three horsemen galloping towards us. When they were about a hundred paces from us, the first dismounted and approached us, limping a little. He was about sixty years old, quite fat (which is rare in this country), with a hard Arabic physiognomy, accentuated, lined, almost ferocious features. He sported the cross of the Legion of Honour. He was called Si Cherif-ben-Vhabeizzi, *caïd* of the Oulad-Dia.

He made a long speech with a furious air, inviting us to come to his tent and have a bite to eat.

It was the first time that I had been inside the tent of a nomadic chief.

A heap of expensive frizzy woollen rugs covered the ground; other rugs were hung up to hide the bare canvass; others were stretched above our heads, forming a thick and impermeable ceiling. Kinds of divans or, rather, thrones, were also covered with admirable fabrics; and a partition made of oriental hangings divided the tent into two equal halves, separating us from the part where the women lived from which we could every now and then distinguish murmuring voices.

We sat down. The two sons of the *caïd* took their place by their father, who himself got up from time to time, saying something underneath the separation to the neighbouring apartment; and an invisible hand passed him steaming dishes that the chief then presented to us.

We could hear small children playing and crying near their mothers. Who were these women? Undoubtedly they were watching us through invisible openings, but we could not see them.

The Arab woman, in general, is small, of milky complexion, with the physiognomy of a young sheep. She only has modesty concerning her face. You encounter some of them going to work with their faces carefully veiled, but their bodies covered only by two strips of wool, one falling in front, and the other behind, allowing, in profile, her whole person to be seen.

From the age of fifteen these poor girls, who would be pretty, are deformed and exhausted by hard work. They toil from morning till night at greatly fatiguing tasks, going several kilometres to look for water with a child on their back. They seem old at twenty-five.

Their face, which is sometimes seen, is tattooed with blue stars on the forehead, cheeks, and chin. The body is depilated, as a measure of cleanliness. The wives of rich Arabs are hardly ever seen.

We set out again as soon as the light meal was over and in the evening we arrived at the salt rock of Khang-el-Melah.

It's a sort of grey, green, blue mountain with metallic glints and strange cuttings—a mountain of salt! Water more salty than the Ocean escapes from its base and, volatilized by the mad heat of the sun, leaves a white scurf behind on the soil, similar to the froth of waves—a foam of salt! You can no longer see the ground, hidden beneath a light powder, as if some giant had amused himself grating this mountain to scatter the dust all about; and large detached blocks lie in the declivities—blocks of salt!

Underneath this extraordinary rock, there are apparently some extremely deep hollowed out wells in which thousands of doves live.

The following day we were at Djelfa.

Djelfa is a small, ugly French town, but it is inhabited by some of the most amiable officers who made it a charming stay.

After a brief rest we continued on our way.

We recommenced our long journey through the long barren plains. From time to time we encountered some flocks. Sometimes these were armies of sand-coloured sheep; sometimes strange beasts took shape on the horizon, rendered small by the distance, and with their humped backs, their great curved necks, and their slow gait, they could be taken for bands of tall turkeys. On nearing them you recognize camels with their stomachs—which can contain up to sixty litres of water—swollen on both sides like a double balloon, like a massive goatskin bottle. They too are the colour of the desert, just as all beings born in these bare, yellow wildernesses are. The lion, the hyena, the jackal, the toad, the lizard, the scorpion, man himself, all take on the shades of the charred soil, from the burning russet of the shifting dunes to the stony grey of the mountains. And the small lark of the plains is so similar in colour to the dust of the earth that you can only see it when it flies away.

The Zar'ez

What do these animals live on in these arid regions, how do they survive?

During the rainy season, these plains are covered in grasses for a few weeks, then in a few days the sun desiccates and burns up this rapid vegetation. And so these plants themselves take on the colour of the soil; they break up and crumble away, scattering across the earth like a finely chopped straw that you can no longer even distinguish. But the herds know how to find it and feed themselves on it. They go about looking for this powder of dried grass. It looks like they are eating stones.

What would a Norman farmer think, faced with these strange pastures?

Next we crossed a region where we hardly even encountered any birds. The wells were becoming untraceable.

We saw passing in the distance strange little columns of dust, a bit like smoke, a few metres high, broad at the summit and thin at the base. Sometimes they were straight, sometimes slanting or twisted as they ran rapidly across the soil.

The eddying of the air, forming a suction, raises up and induces these transparent and quite fantastic clouds, which are the only things that move in these lamentably deserted places.

Five hundred metres ahead of our small troop, a rider being used as a guide directed us through the dull wilderness in front. For ten minutes he went at walking pace, motionless on his saddle, and singing in his language, a languid song, with strange rhythms. We copied his pace. Then suddenly he left at a trot, barely stirring, his big burnous flying, the body upright, standing up in the stirrups. And we went off after him until he would stop and once more resume a slower rate.

I asked my neighbour:

'How can he lead us across these bare spaces with no points of reference?'

He answered:

'There are always the bones of camels.'

In fact every quarter of an hour or so we came across some enormous bones, gnawed by animals, cooked by the sun and turned very white, stains in the sand. Sometimes there was a piece of leg, sometimes a piece of jawbone, sometimes the end of a spinal column.

'Where does all this debris come from?' I asked.

My neighbour retorted:

'En route, convoys leave behind the animals that can no longer follow; and the jackals don't carry everything away.'

And for several days we continued this monotonous journey, behind the same Arab, in the same order, always on horseback, almost without speaking.

Now, one afternoon, when we had to reach Bou-Saada by evening, I noticed very far in front of us a brown mass, enlarged by the mirage, and whose form astonished me. On our approach two vultures flew away. It was a decaying carcass, still all slobbery in spite of the heat, varnished by rotten blood. The chest alone remained, the limbs without doubt having been carried off by the voracious devourers of the dead.

'We have some travellers in front of us,' said the lieutenant.

A few hours after this we entered into a kind of ravine or mountain pass. It was like a frightful furnace, with jagged rocks like the teeth of a saw, pointed, seeming angry and indignant against the backdrop of the pitilessly ferocious sky. Another body lay there. A jackal that was devouring it fled.

Then, just where it opened up again on to the plain, a grey mass, stretched out in front of us, stirring, and slowly, at the end of a great neck, I saw the head of a dying camel raise itself. He had been there, on his side, for two or three days perhaps, dying of tiredness and thirst. His long limbs were lying on the fiery soil, inert, mangled, and looking like they were broken. Hearing us coming, he had raised his head up, like a beacon. His forehead, corroded by the inexorable sun, was now only one big, weeping wound; and his resigned eyes followed us. He did not utter a groan, he didn't make an effort to get up. It was as if he knew, having seen plenty of his brothers die on his lengthy travels across these wildernesses, he knew well the inclemency of men. It was his turn, that was all. We passed by.

Turning around a long while afterwards, I could still see, raised up from the sand, the long neck of this abandoned beast watching till the end, the last living beings it would see, disappearing over the horizon.

One hour later, there was a dog cowering against a rock, mouth open, fangs gleaming, incapable of moving a paw, its gaze held by two vultures nearby, preening their feathers as they awaited his death. It was so overcome with fear of these patient animals, eager for his flesh, that he didn't turn his head or feel the stones that a spahi threw at him in passing.

And suddenly, at the exit of another mountain pass, I noticed the oasis in front of me.

It's an unforgettable sight. You have just crossed interminable plains, cleared sharp-pointed mountains, peeled and charred terrain, without passing a single tree, plant, or green leaf, and then here, in front of you, right at your feet, an opaque mass of dark verdure, something akin to a lake of almost black foliage spread out on the sand. Then behind this big blot the desert begins again, stretching out into infinity, as far as the forever out of reach horizon, where it blends in with the sky.

The town slopes down as far as the gardens.

What towns, these cities of the Sahara! An agglomeration, a heap of mud bricks dried under the sun. All these square huts of hardened mud are pressed one against the other in a way that leaves between their meandering rows kinds of narrow galleries which serve as streets, and resemble those tracks that mark out the regular passages of animals.

The entire city, moreover, this poor city of thinned out earth, gives the impression of being the construction of some kind of animal, like the dams of beavers, unshapely works built without tools, instead built only with those means that nature has left to creatures of an inferior order.

Here and there a magnificent palm tree opens out twenty feet from the ground. Suddenly you enter into a forest in which the alleyways are enclosed between two high clay walls. To left and right a population of date trees open their large parasols above the gardens, sheltering with their deep and fresh shade the delicate throng of fruit trees. Under the protection of these giant palms, which the wind shakes like broad fans, sprout vines, apricot trees, fig trees, pomegranates, and invaluable vegetables.

The water of the river, kept in large reservoirs, is distributed among the properties like gas is in our country. A severe administration keeps account of what each inhabitant uses, the water being dispensed from the source by means of runnels for one or two hours a week according to the extent of the property.

Wealth is estimated by the number of palm trees. These trees, guardians of life, protect the saplings, their roots are always plunged in water, whilst their crowns are bathed in fire.

The valley of Bou-Saada which leads the river to the gardens is marvellous, like a dreamscape. It descends, full of date trees, fig trees, big, magnificent plants, between two mountains whose summits are red. All along the rapid course of water female Arabs, with their heads veiled and their legs uncovered, wash their linen, dancing over it. They roll it into heaps in the current, and they beat it with their bare feet, balancing gracefully.

Along this ravine the stream runs and sings. On leaving the oasis it is still abundant; but the desert awaits it and, at the doors of the gardens, the yellow, thirsty desert all of a sudden drinks it up, brusquely swallowing it in its sterile sands.

Climbing up to the mosque at sunset to contemplate the whole of this town, it has a most unique appearance. The flat and square roofs form a kind of cascade of muddy draughtboards or dirty handkerchiefs. And on these the whole population moves about, climbing on to the roofs of their huts as soon as evening comes. On the streets nobody is seen, nothing is heard; but once you discover that all the roofs of the town form an elevated extension to the place, you will discover an extraordinary commotion. Supper is prepared. Bunches of children in white rags swarm in the corners; the unshapely bundle of dirty linen that represents the common female Arab cooks the couscous, or gets on with some work.

Night falls. And so the rugs from Djebel-Amour are stretched out on the roofs, having carefully hunted out the scorpions that proliferate in these hovels; then the whole family goes to sleep in the open air under the twinkling swarm of stars.

The oasis of Bou-Saada, although small, is one of the most charming places in Algeria. In the surrounding areas you can hunt the gazelle, which is found there in quantity. An abundance of those formidable *léfaas* are also found there, and also the hideous tarantula with its long legs, whose enormous shadow is seen running along the walls of the huts in the evenings.

Quite a considerable amount of business is done in this *ksar*, because it is found on the road of Mzab.

The Mozabites and the Jews are the only merchants, the only traders, the only industrious beings in all this part of Africa.

As you go further south, the Jewish race takes on a hideous appearance which makes the ferocious hatred certain peoples have against these people, and even the recent massacres, seem understandable. The Jews of Europe, the Jews of Algiers, the Jews that we know, that we mingle with every day, our neighbours and our friends, are men of the world, educated, intelligent and often charming. And we become violently indignant when we learn that the inhabitants of some small and distant unknown town have slit the throats and drowned a few hundred of the children of Israel. I am no longer so shocked today; for our Jews do not resemble the Jews over there.[16]

At Bou-Saada, you see them, squatting in their filthy dens, bloated with grease, sordid, awaiting the Arab, as a spider waits for a fly. They call him [the Arab], they try to lend him a hundred sous against a bill that he will sign. The man knows the danger, hesitates, doesn't want to. But the desire to drink, and other desires, continue to tug at him. A hundred sous represents for him so many pleasures!

At last he gives in, takes the piece of silver, and signs the greasy paper.

At the end of three months he owes ten francs, one hundred francs at the end of a year, two hundred francs after three years. And then the Jew sells his land, if he has any, or if not, his camel, his horse, his donkey, finally all that he owns.

The chiefs, the *Caïds*, Aghas or Bach'aghas, fall just as easily into the claws of these rapacious beings who are the blight, the bleeding wound, of our colony, and the great obstacle to the civilization and well-being of the Arab.

When a French column goes to raid some rebel tribe, a cloud of Jews follows it, buying at a dirt cheap price the booty which they then sell back to the Arabs as soon as the army corps has moved away.

If, for example, six thousand sheep are seized in a region, what's to be done with the animals? Drive them to the towns? They would die on the way, for how do you feed them, how do you get them to drink when you have to cross two or three hundred kilometres of bare land? And then to move and look after such a convoy you would need double the original troops.

So do you kill them? What a massacre and what a waste! And then the Jews are there asking to buy at two francs each the sheep which are worth twenty. Well, at least the treasury will earn twelve thousand francs. And so they give them to them.

Eight days later the first owners take their sheep back at three francs a head. French vengeance is not expensive.

The Jew is master of the whole south of Algeria. There are hardly any Arabs, in fact, who do not have a debt, because they do not like to pay back. They prefer to renew their tickets at a hundred or two hundred per cent. They always believe they are saved if they gain themselves some time. There needs to be a special law to change this deplorable situation.

Throughout the South, for that matter, the Jew practises nothing but usury by the most underhand methods possible; the true merchants are the Mozabites.

Arriving in a village somewhere in the Sahara, you immediately notice a particular race of men who have taken hold of the business of the region. They alone have shops; shops which have both European merchandise and that from local industry; they are intelligent, active, merchants to their very core. They are the Beni-Mzab or Mozabites. They are nicknamed the 'Jews of the desert'.

The Arab, the real Arab, the man of the tents, for whom all work is dishonourable, despises the commercial Mozabite; but he comes at regular intervals to stock up from his shop; he confers to him precious objects that he cannot keep on his wandering life. A kind of steadfast pact is established between them.

The Mozabites have therefore monopolized all trade in North Africa. They are found as much in our towns as they are in Saharan villages. When the merchant has made his fortune, he returns to Mzab, where he has to undergo a sort of purification before being able to resume his political rights.

These Arabs, recognizable from their size—they are smaller and bulkier than those of other tribes, often having flat, broad faces and strong lips, with their eyes generally sunk under straight and bushy eyebrows—are schismatic Muslims. They belong to one of the three dissenting sects of North Africa and seem, to certain scholars, to be the current descendants of the former sectarians of Kharijism. [17]

The country of these men is perhaps the strangest on African soil.

Their fathers, driven out of Syria by the weaponry of the Prophet, then came to live in the Djebel-Nefoussa, to the west of Tripoli in Barbary.

But successively pushed back from every place that they settled, envied everywhere for their intelligence and industry, and treated with suspicion for their heterodoxy, they finally stopped in the most arid, burning and awful region of all. In Arabic it is called Hammada (heated) and Chebka (mesh) because it resembles a great mesh of rocks and black rubble.

The country of the Mozabites is situated about one hundred and fifty kilometres from Laghouat.

Here is how Commander Coÿne, the man who knows the whole of southern Algeria the best, describes, in a most interesting booklet, his arrival in Mzab: [18]

The Zar'ez

Not far from the centre of the Chebka is found a sort of amphitheatre formed by a belt of very bright limestone rocks and very steep slopes on the interior. It is opened on the north-west and on the south-east by two trenches which let the Oued-Mzab pass. This amphitheatre is about eighteen kilometres in length with a breadth of two or more kilometres, it encloses five towns of the confederation of the Mzab,[19] and the lands are cultivated exclusively as gardens for the inhabitants of this valley.

Viewed from the exterior of the north and eastern sides, this belt of rocks appears like an agglomeration of *koubbas*[20] laid out in tiers, piled one on top of the other, in no particular order; it could be described as a great Arab necropolis. The eye finds no trace of vegetation there; the birds of prey themselves seem to flee these desolate regions. Only the rays of the implacable sun reflect on these walls of grey-white rocks, producing from their shadows fantastic patterns.

The astonishment, I will even say the enthusiasm, of the traveller is immense when he arrives on the crest of this line of rocks, and discovers on the interior of the amphitheatre five populous towns surrounded by gardens of luxurious vegetation standing out in dark green upon the reddish bottom of the bed of the Oued-Mzab.

About him is the denuded desert, death; at his feet, life, and the evident proofs of an advanced civilization.

The Mzab is a republic, or rather a commune, similar to those that the Parisian revolutionaries tried to establish in 1871.[21]

Nobody in Mzab has the right to remain inactive; and the child, as soon as he can walk and carry something, helps his father water the gardens which form the constant and greatest occupation of the inhabitants. From morning to night, the mule or camel draws in the leather bucket of water which is immediately poured into a runnel, ingeniously organized in a way that not a single drop of this precious liquid is lost.

The Mzab have in addition a great number of dams to store the rains. It is thus infinitely more advanced than our Algeria.

The rain! It brings happiness, confers comfort and saves the harvest for the Mozabite; as soon as it falls, a kind of madness seizes the inhabitants. They go out on to the streets, fire their rifles, sing, run to the gardens, to the river which begins to flow again, and to the dykes, the upkeep of which is maintained by each citizen. As soon as a dyke is threatened, everyone must take themselves off there.

And these people, through their constant work, their industry and their wisdom, have made there, out of the wildest and most desolate part of the Sahara, a living, settled, cultivated country, where seven prosperous towns are spread out under the sun.[22] The Mozabite is protective of his fatherland, he defends it as much as possible from the entrance of Europeans. In certain towns, such as Beni-Isguem, no foreigner has the right to spend even one night there.

The police is formed from everyone. Nobody would refuse to lend a strong hand where necessary. In this country there are neither any poor nor any beggars. The needy are fed by their own people.

Nearly everyone knows how to read and write.

Everywhere there are schools, considerable communal establishments. And a lot of Mozabites, after having spent a while in our towns, return home, knowing French, Spanish and Italian.

Commander Coÿne's booklet contains countless numbers of surprising details on these curious little people.

At Bou-Saada, like in all the oases and all the towns, there are Mozabites doing business, making exchanges, owning all sorts of shops, and applying themselves to all professions.

After four days spent in this little Saharan city, I headed back for the coast.

The mountains, encountered on the way back to the coast, had a strange appearance. They resembled monstrous, strong castles with crenellations stretching on for kilometres. They are regular, square, cut in a mathematical way. The highest is flat and seems inaccessible. That shape has given it the nickname 'the Billiard Table'. Shortly before my arrival, two officers climbed it for the first time. On the summit they found two enormous Roman cisterns.[23]

VIII

Kabylie - Bougie

Here we have the richest and most populated part of Algeria. The country of the Kabyles is mountainous and covered with forests and fields.

On leaving Aumale, you descend towards the great valley of Sahel.

There stands an immense mountain, the Djurjura. Its higher peaks are grey, as if they were covered with ashes.

All around, on the less elevated summits, villages are seen which, from afar, appear like heaps of white stones. Others are hitched on to the slopes. Throughout this fertile region the battle between the European and the native for the possession of land is terrible.

Kabylie is more populated than the most densely inhabited département in France. The Kabyles are not nomads, but sedentary and hard-working. However, the *Algérien* [1] has no other preoccupation than to dispossess them.

Here are the different systems employed to drive out and despoil the poor indigenous owners.

Any private individual, leaving France, will request from the office in charge of the distribution of land a concession in Algeria. He is presented with a hat with some bits of paper in it, and he pulls out a number corresponding to a plot of land. This plot, from now on, belongs to him.

He leaves. He finds over there, in a native village, a whole family settled on the concession that had been designated to him. This family have brought the land into cultivation, are attuned to it, because it is upon this land that they live.

They own nothing else. The foreigner expels them. They go, resigned, since *it is the French law*. But now these people, henceforth without any resources, reach the desert and become rebels.

In other instances they come to an arrangement. The European colonist, scared off by the heat and appearance of this country, enters into talks with the Kabyle, who becomes his farmer.

And the native remains on *his* land, sending, be it a good year or a bad year, fifteen hundred or two thousand francs, to the European who has returned to France.

That is an equivalent concession to that of a tobacconist's.

Another method.

The Chamber votes a credit of forty or fifty million intended for the colonization of Algeria.

What should be done with this money? Surely dams should be built, trees planted on the mountain summits to retain water, endeavours should be made to render these sterile plains fertile?

By no means. The Arab is expropriated. Now, in Kabylie, the land has acquired a considerable value. The best places fetch SIXTEEN HUNDRED FRANCS A HECTARE; and it is generally sold for eight hundred francs. The Kabyles, the owners, live tranquilly on their cultivations. Rich, they do not revolt; they ask for nothing more than to be left in peace.

What happens? Fifty million to spend? Kabylie is the most beautiful area of Algeria. Oh well! the Kabyles are expropriated for the profit of unknown colonists.

But how are they expropriated? They are paid FORTY FRANCS a hectare for land worth, at the minimum, EIGHT HUNDRED FRANCS.

And the chief of the family goes without saying anything (it's the law) it doesn't matter where, with his people, his men, women and children all at loose ends.

These people are neither commercial, nor industrial, only farmers.

So the family lives as long as something remains of the derisory sum given to them. Then poverty arrives. The men take up arms and follow someone like Bou-Amama, which proves once again that Algeria can only be governed by a military officer.

They say: 'We leave the native in the fertile parts as long as we lack Europeans; then, when they [Europeans] come, we expropriate the first occupant.' 'Very well.

Kabylie - Bougie

But when you no longer have any fertile areas, what will you do then?' 'We will fertilize, by Jove!' 'Ah right! Why don't you fertilize immediately, since you have fifty million?'

How, when you see certain companies creating gigantic dams to supply water to entire regions; when you know that through the remarkable works of talented engineers, it would be sufficient to afforest a few summits to gain leagues of land stretching out below, how then is it you cannot find another method than that of expelling the Kabyles!

It is pertinent to add that once the Tell is crossed, the land becomes bare, arid and almost impossible to cultivate. Only the Arab, who can subsist on two handfuls of flour and a few figs each day, can survive in these desiccated regions. The European cannot make his living here. Therefore, in reality, there only remain restricted spaces in which to install the colonists, unless one. . . . . drives out the natives. And that's what is done.

Overall, apart from the fortunate proprietors on the Mitidja Plain, those who have obtained lands in Kabylie through one of the processes that I have just described, and those who are settled along the coast in the narrow band of land that the Atlas [Mountains] demarcate, the colonists scream of poverty. And Algeria can no longer take in more than a fairly low number from abroad. She cannot feed them.

This colony, besides, is infinitely difficult to govern, for reasons easy to comprehend.

As big as a kingdom in Europe, Algeria is formed of very diverse regions, which are inhabited by essentially different populations. This is what no government so far has seemed to understand.

A thorough knowledge of each region must be had to claim governance over it, for each region has a need for its own particular laws, regulations, measures and precautions. However, the governor, whatever he be, absolutely and fatally ignores these matters of details and customs [*moeurs*]; he can only refer to the administrators who represent him.

What are these administrators? Colonists? People raised in the country, au fait with all its needs? By no means! They are simply youngsters from Paris in the retinue of the viceroy.[2]

And so one of these young ignoramuses ends up governing fifty or a hundred thousand men. He makes gaff after gaff and ruins the country. It's to be expected.

There are exceptions. Sometimes the all-powerful governor's delegate works, seeks to inform himself and to understand. It would take him ten years to even begin to be anywhere near up to speed. Then at the end of six months he is changed. He is sent for family reasons, or personal convenience or some such, from the Tunisian border to the Moroccan border; and there he immediately sets about governing with the same methods he employed previously, trusting in his newfound experience, and applying the same rules and procedures to an essentially different population.

So, it's not a good governor that we need above all else, but for the governor to have a good entourage.

To remedy this deplorable state of affairs, these disastrous customs, an attempt was made to create a school of administration where basic principles, essential for leading this country, would be ingrained in a whole class of young people. It failed. The entourage of M. Albert Grévy aborted this project. Favouritism once again had the victory.[3]

The personnel of the administrators are thus recruited in a more unique way. You will find here, it is true, a few intelligent and hard-working men. But in the end, short of capable candidates, the government promoted former officers of the *bureaux arabes*. They at least knew the natives well; but it can hardly be said that their change of costume immediately changed their principles of administration; and it doesn't do to drive them out with fury when they wear the uniform, in order to take them back as soon as they are reclothed in frock coats.

Since I've let myself broach the difficult subject of the administration of Algeria, I want to say a few more words on a question of great import whose solution should be swiftly determined; it's the question of the great native chiefs, who in reality are the only administrators, the all-powerful administrators of all that part of our colony comprised between the Tell and the desert.

At the start of the French occupation, the chiefs who offered the greatest guarantee of fidelity were invested with the titles of Aghas or Bach'Aghas, with a widespread authority over the tribes of a great swathe of the territory. Any action of ours would have lacked power;[4] so we brought in Arab chiefs won over to our cause, all the while resigning ourselves in advance to possible betrayals; and they were rather frequent. The measure was wise, diplomatic; it gave, on the whole, excellent results. Certain Aghas rendered us considerable services and, thanks to them, the lives of, perhaps, several thousand French soldiers were saved.

But although a measure might have been excellent at a given moment, it doesn't follow that it will remain perfect, regardless of all the modifications that time brings to a country in the process of colonization.

Today, the presence among the tribes of these potentates, who alone are respected and obeyed, is the cause of a considerable danger to us, and an insurmountable obstacle to the civilization of the Arabs. However, the military party seems to vigorously defend the system of native chiefs against the tendencies of the civil party to suppress them.

I could not treat this serious question; but completing the excursion I made among the tribes was sufficient to see clearly the enormous inconveniences of the current situation. I simply want to quote some facts.

The lengthy resistance of Bou-Amama is almost solely down to the agha of Saïda.

At the beginning of this insurrection, this agha, with his *goums*, went to join up with the French column. He met the Trafis on the way, who had been summoned with the same intention, and he joined them.

But the agha of Saïda is loaded with debts that he cannot pay. Now the idea doubtlessly came to him during the night to gather his *goum* and make a raid and descend upon the Trafis. The latter were beaten by the first attack, but then regained the advantage; and the agha of Saïda was constrained to flee with his men.

Now, as the agha of Saïda is our ally, our friend and our lieutenant, as he represents French authority, the Trafis were convinced that we had a hand in the affair; and, instead of joining up with the French camp, they defected and immediately went to find Bou-Amama, with whom they remained, constituting his principal force.

A characteristic example, is it not? And the agha of Saïda stays our faithful friend. He marches under our banners!

To quote another example, there is a famous agha[5] whom our military heads treat with great consideration because of his considerable influence which prevails over a great number of tribes.

Sometimes he helps us, sometimes he betrays us, whichever is to his advantage. Openly allied to the French, from whom he holds authority, he secretly supports all the uprisings. It's fair to say that he indifferently drops his ties to one or other party as soon as a possibility of pillaging arises.

After having played an undeniable part in the assassination of Colonel Beauprêtre,[6] today he is marching with us. But he is strongly suspected of having something to do with the many miscalculations we have undertaken.

Our unshakeable ally, the agha of Frenda,[7] has warned us many times of the double-crossing of this potentate. But we have closed our ears, because he himself [Frenda?] only renders the same self-interested services to the military authorities as he does to our enemies.

This particular situation, the open protection we accord to this chief [the 'famous' agha], assures him of impunity for a multitude of misdemeanours that he commits daily.

This is what happens.

Arabs, throughout Algeria, steal from one another. There isn't a night where we aren't told about twenty stolen camels on this side, a hundred sheep on that side, oxen lifted from Biskra, horses from Djelfa. The thieves always remain untraceable. Nevertheless there isn't an officer of the *bureau arabe* who is ignorant of where the stolen cattle goes to! It goes to this agha [the 'famous' agha] who acts as a receiver of stolen goods to all the bandits of the desert. The filched animals are mixed up with his immense herds; he takes a cut for his complaisance, and returns the rest after a while, when the danger of prosecution has passed.

Nobody in the South is unaware of this situation.

But we need this man, whom we have allowed to build up a great influence, increased each day through the help he gives to all these marauders; and so we turn a blind eye.

To top it all off, this chief is incalculably wealthy, whilst, for example, the agha of Djelfa has been partly ruined in serving the interests of colonization, in building farms, clearing the land, etc.

Now apart from this list of facts, a crowd of other more serious drawbacks result from the presence of these native potentates among the tribes. To give a good account of it, you need to have an intimate understanding of Algeria today.

The territory and the population of our colony are divided in a very clear way.

First off there are the coastal towns which have no more relations with the interior of Algeria than French towns have with this colony.

The inhabitants of the coastal Algerian towns are essentially sedentary; they do nothing but feel the side effects of what happens in the interior, but their action on Arab territory is absolutely nil.

The second zone, the Tell, is partly occupied by European colonists. Now, the colonist only sees the Arab as an enemy with whom he is going to have disputes over land. He hates him instinctively, pursues him ceaselessly, and fleeces him when he can. The Arab reciprocates.

The bellicose hostility between the Arabs and the colonists thus prevents the latter from having any civilizing effect on the former. In this region things are still only half-bad. The European element unceasingly tending to eliminate the native element, it won't be long before the Arab, ruined or dispossessed, will take refuge further south.

Now it is essential that these conquered neighbours always remain peaceful. For that, it is necessary that our authority is exerted over them at every moment, that our action is ceaseless, and that our influence prevails above all.

What happens today?

The tribes, dispersed over a great expanse of land, never come into contact with the Europeans. Only the officers from the *bureaux* [*arabes*] make, from time to time, a tour of inspection, contenting themselves with asking the *caïds* how things are going in their tribe.

But the *caïd* is placed under the authority of the native chief, the agha or the bach'agha. If the chief is *de grande tente*, of an illustrious family respected across the desert, well, his authority is limitless. All the *caïds* obey him just as they would have done before the French occupation; and none of what goes on ever reaches the knowledge of the military authorities.

The tribe is still, then, a closed world, because of the fear and respect that the agha instils, because he continues the traditions of his ancestors, exercising all kinds of exactions on his Arab subjects. He is the master, making them hand over whatever he wants, sometimes a hundred sheep, sometimes two hundred, behaving like a little tyrant; and, as he holds his authority from us, it's a continuation of the former Arab regime under the French government, hierarchical theft, etc., and without realizing it we are completely unaware of the true state of the country and how little we count for.

It is solely down to this situation that we always have so little awareness of any revolts until the moment they break out.

So, the presence of the great native chiefs indefinitely removes any real and direct influence the French authorities have over the tribes, who remain to us a closed world.

The remedy? Here it is. Nearly all of the chiefs, except two or three, need money. They must be given a private income of ten, twenty, or thirty thousand francs a year—because of their influence and for services that they have formerly rendered us—and be constrained to living in either Algiers, or in another coastal town. Some soldiers claim an insurrection would follow this measure. They have their reasons...familiar ones. Other officers living in the interior, on the contrary, assert that this would be appeasement.

But that's not everything. These men would have to be replaced with civil servants who would live in the tribes all the time, exacting a direct authority over the *caïds*. This way, little by little, civilization would enter into these regions, once this big obstacle of the native chiefs was pushed aside.

But useful reforms are a long time coming in Algeria, just as they are in France.

In crossing Kabylie I had experience of the complete impotence of our actions even among the tribes who live amidst Europeans.

I went towards the sea, following the long valley that leads from Beni-Mansour to Bougie. In front of us, in the distance, a strange thick cloud closed off the horizon. Overhead the sky was the milky blue colour that it takes in the summer in these hot regions; but, over there, a brown cloud with yellow highlights—which seemed to be neither a storm, nor a fog, nor one of those thick sandstorms that pass with the fury of a hurricane—was shrouding the whole country in its grey shadow. This heavy, opaque cloud, almost black at its base and lighter in the heights of the sky, barred, like a wall, the broad valley. And all of a sudden there seemed to be a vague odour of burnt wood in the motionless air. But what gigantic fire could produce this mountain of smoke?

Indeed it was smoke. All the Kabyle forests had caught on fire.

We soon entered into this suffocating semi-darkness. You couldn't see more than a hundred metres in front of you. The horses were breathing heavily. It seemed as though evening had come; and a light breeze, one of those slow breezes that barely rustle the leaves, was pushing this floating night towards the sea.

We waited two hours in a village for news; then our little carriage set off on its way again, with the true night now, in its turn, stretching out over the earth.

A dim, still distant, glimmer lit up the sky like a meteor. It grew and it grew, rising up in front of the horizon, more bloody than brilliant. Then with a sudden turning in the valley, I thought I was opposite an immense, illuminated town. It was an entire mountain, already burnt up. The undergrowth had cooled down, but the trunks of the oaks and olive trees were still incandescent, like enormous coals. Standing in their thousands, no longer smoking, they were like throngs of colossal lights. It all resembled a city lit up in the night and seen from a distance: lights, aligned or scattered, marking out the random or ordered amalgamation of great boulevards, squares, and winding streets.

As we went along we got closer to the big fire, and the light became dazzling. During this one day the flames had swept through twenty kilometres of wood.

When I saw the blaze, I remained terrified and delighted in front of the most terrible and most captivating spectacle that I had ever seen. The fire, like a wave, broke over an incalculable width. It was razing the country, advancing unceasingly and rapidly. The undergrowth flared and went out. Like torches, the big trees burned slowly, creating high plumes of fire, whilst the short flames of the brushwood galloped ahead.

All night we followed this monstrous inferno. As day was breaking we reached the sea.

Enclosed by a belt of strange mountains—with strange and charming, jagged crests and wooded flanks—was the gulf of Bougie. The gulf was a creamy yet limpid blue, incredibly transparent, filling out under the azure of the sky, that unchanging azure that you might say was fixed.

At the end of the coast, on the left, on the steep slope of a mountain, in a bed of greenery, the town rolls down towards the sea in a stream of white houses.

When you enter it, it comes across like one of those sweet and incredible cities from the opera, of which you sometimes dream in hallucinations of unreal countries.

There are Moorish houses, French houses, and ruins everywhere, like the ruins you see in the foreground of stage scenery, opposite a cardboard palace.

On arriving, standing near the sea, above the quay—where the transatlantic liners approach, where the fishing boats with their sails like wings are tied—in the midst of a real fairytale landscape, you come across a ruin so magnificent that it doesn't seem natural. It's the old Saracen gate, overgrown with ivy.[8]

And in the hilly woods about the city, there are ruins everywhere, sections of Roman walls, pieces of Saracen monuments, remainders of Arabic constructions.

The day slipped by, peaceful and burning, then night came. And all about us, all around the gulf was an amazing sight. As the shadows thickened another glimmer, like that of day, began to invade the horizon. The fire, like a besieging army, surrounded the town, drawing closer around it. New fires, lit by the Kabyles, were appearing in rapid succession, wondrously reflected in the calm waters of the vast basin which was surrounded by coasts set ablaze. The fire sometimes appeared like a garland of Chinese lanterns,[9] or like a snake with rings of flame twisting and crawling along the undulations of the mountain, or sometimes gushing like a volcanic eruption, with a glaring centre and an immense plume of red smoke, according to whether it consumed the spread out plantations of brushwood or the wood of full-grown trees.

I stayed for six days in this flaming land, then I left by the incomparable road which circumvents the gulf and goes alongside the mountains, overlooked by some forests, and overlooking in turn other forests and endless sand dunes; the golden sands lapped by the peaceful waves of the Mediterranean.

Sometimes the fire reached the path. We had to jump out of the carriage to clear away burning trees that had fallen down in front of us; sometimes, four horses galloping, we went between two waves of fire, one descending to the bottom of a ravine where a big torrent flowed, the other climbing up to the summits, eating away at the mountain, exposing her bare russet skin. The burnt hills, extinguished and cooled down, seemed to be covered in a black veil, a veil of mourning.

Sometimes we crossed regions that were still untouched. The anxious colonists, standing in their doorways, asked us for news of the fire, in the same way that in France, at the time of the German war,[10] people asked for information about the movements of the enemy.

We saw jackals, hyenas, foxes, hares, hundreds of different animals, fleeing in front of the scourge, thrown into a panic by the terror of the flame.

At a turning into a valley I suddenly saw five telegraph wires so loaded with swallows that they bowed strangely, forming between each post, five garlands of birds.

But the coachman cracked his big whip. A cloud of creatures flew off, scattering in the air; and the fat iron wires, suddenly relieved, bounced up, slackening like the string of a bow. They trembled for a long time after, shaken by long vibrations that calmed little by little.

Soon we entered into the gorges of Chabet-el-Akhra. Leaving the sea on the left, we entered into the half-opened mountain. The passage is one of the most grandiose that you can see. The cutting often narrows; bare granite peaks—reddish, brown or blue—close in, leaving only a thin passage at their base for the water; and the road is no more than a narrow cornice cut into the rock itself, just above the flowing torrent.

The appearance of this arid gorge, wild and wonderful, is constantly changing. The two walls which enclose it sometimes rise up nearly two thousand metres; and the sun cannot penetrate to the bottom of this well except when it is directly above it.

At the entrance on the other side, you arrive at the village of Kerrata. For eight days the inhabitants have watched black smoke from the fire come out of the dark defile like a gigantic chimney.

After this disastrous blow, which could easily have been prevented with a little foresight and effort, the government of Algeria claimed that the fire had not been started by the Kabyles. They also said that the forests that were burnt down consisted of no more than fifty thousand hectares.

First off, here is a dispatch from the sub-prefect of Philippeville.

> *I was informed by the mayor and administrator of Jemmapes*[11] *that all forestry concessions have been reduced to nothing and that the fire ravaged all the* douars *of the* commune mixte; *the villages of Gastu, Aïn-Cherchar, and le Djendel were threatened.*
>
> *At Philippeville, all the wooded massifs were burnt.*
>
> *Stora, Saint-Antoine, Valée and Damrémont escaped becoming prey to the flames.*
>
> *At El-Arrouch, little damage outside of the five hundred hectares burnt in the* douars *of the Oulad-Messaoud, Hazabra and El-Ghedir.*
>
> *At Saint-Charles, approximately six hundred hectares burnt between the Oued-Deb and the Oued-Goudi, and eight hundred hectares to the north-east and the south-east. Fodder and gourbis destroyed.*[12]
>
> *At Collo mixte and Attia, the fire ravaged everything.*
>
> *The Teissier, Lesseps, Levat, Lefebvre, Sider, Bessin, etc. concessions were either completely or partially destroyed. A further forty thousand hectares of state-owned woods. The farms and houses of Zériban were devoured by the flames. Numerous human victims have been counted.*

This morning we have buried three dead Zouaves, victims of their devotion to duty near Valée.

The damages are incalculable and cannot even approximately be evaluated.

The danger disappeared, largely after all the woods had been destroyed. The wind also changed direction, and I think that we can gain control over the last fires, notably in the Besson and Collo properties, and at l'Estaya near Robertville.

Yesterday I sent a troop of a hundred and fifty men to Collo, by requisitioning a transatlantic passenger ship.

We can add the fires of the forests of Zeramna, Fil-Fila, Fendeck, etc., to those above.

M. Bisern, contractor of the El-Milia forests for fourteen years wrote this:

My staff exhibited the greatest energy. They were very gravely exposed, and twice we had gained control over the fire. But to no purpose. Whilst we fought the fire on one side, the Arabs relit it on the other, in several different places.

Here is a letter from a proprietor:

I have the honour of announcing to you that, towards the middle of Sunday-Monday night, my farmer, Ripeyre, on guard on my property located above the parade ground, saw four attempts at arson: in the communal ground; a few hundred metres from my property; another above Damrémont; and the fourth above Valée. The wind lacking, the fire couldn't spread.

Here is a dispatch from Djidjelli:

Djidjelli, August 23, 3.16 a.m.

The fire ravaged the forestry concession of Beni-Amram, belonging to M. Carpentier, Édouard, from Djidjelli.

Last night it was lit in twenty different places; a roadmender, arriving from the mine at Cavalho, distinctly saw all the fires.

> *This morning, almost under the eyes of* caïd Amar-ben-Habilès, *of the Beni-Foughal tribe, the fire was put to the canton of Mezrech; and a quarter of an hour later the fire had taken up at another part of the same canton, in the opposite direction of the wind.*
>
> *Finally, at the same time, four hundred paces from a group formed by the caïd and about fifty Arabs from his tribe, still in the opposite direction to the wind, a new outbreak of fire sparked up.*
>
> *It is therefore quite obvious that the fire was spread by the native population, and in execution of a given order.*

I will add that, having myself spent six days in the middle of this country set afire, I saw, with my own eyes, in one night, the fire break out simultaneously in eight different spots in the middle of the woods, ten kilometres from any dwellings.

It is certain that if we exert an active surveillance over the tribes, that these disasters, which reoccur every four or five years, would not take place.

The government believed it had done what was necessary when, as the hot season drew nearer, it renewed the instructions concerning the establishment of watchtower posts instituted by article 4 of the law of July 17, 1874. This article is worded as follows:

> The native populations, in the forested areas, will be, during the period from the 1st of July to the 1st of November, bound, under the penalties decreed in article 8, to a surveillance service, which will be regulated by the governor general.

We suspect the natives of wanting to set the forests on fire. . .and we entrust them to keep watch over them!

Is this not a monumental naïveté?

This article was without doubt punctually executed. Every native was at his post. . . only. . .he set it on fire.

Another article, it is true, prescribed a special surveillance to be exercised by an officer designated each year by the governor general.

This article was never received, or almost never carried out.

Let us add that the forestry administration, perhaps the most troublesome of all Algerian administrations, in general does all that is necessary to exasperate the natives.

Finally, to summarize the question of colonization, the government, in order to support the establishment of Europeans, employs with respect to the Arabs absolutely iniquitous methods. Why should the colonists not follow an example which agrees so well with their interests?

It must be noted, however, that for several years, some very capable men, with great expertise in all matters of culture, seem to have placed the colony into an appreciably better state. Algeria is becoming productive under the efforts of those latest arrivals. The population which is taking shape no longer works only for personal interests, but also for French interests.

It is certain that the land, in the hands of these men, will yield what it has never yielded in the hands of the Arabs; it is also certain that the primitive population will disappear little by little; it is undoubted that this disappearance will be extremely useful for Algeria, but it is revolting that it takes place under the conditions in which it is being achieved.

IX

Constantine

From Chabet as far as Sétif you believe you are crossing a golden country. The harvests cut high, not mown close-cropped as in France, crushed by the feet of the herds, mixing the light yellow of the straw with the darker red of the soil, just give the earth that warm, rich tint of old gildings.

Sétif is one of the ugliest towns you can see.

Then, as far as Constantine, you cross interminable plains. The clumps of greenery, from place to place, make it resemble a pine table on which Nuremberg trees have been scattered.[1]

And here is Constantine, the phenomenal city, the strange Constantine, watched over by a snake writhing at its feet, the Roumel, the fantastic Roumel, the river of a poem you might have thought dreamt up by Dante, river of hell running at the bottom of a red abyss, as if the eternal flames had burned it.[2] This jealous and surprising river makes an island of its town; it surrounds it with a terrible and tortuous chasm, with dazzling and bizarre rocks, with upright and jagged walls.

The Arabs say that the city has the appearance of a stretched out burnous. They call it Belad-el-Haoua, the city of air, the city of the ravine, the city of passions. She overlooks admirable valleys full of Roman ruins, aqueducts with giant archways, valleys also full of a marvellous vegetation. She is overlooked by the heights of Mansoura and Sidi-Meçid.[3]

She appears to be standing upright on her rock, guarded by her river, like a queen. An old saying glorifies her: 'Bless the memory of your ancestors,' it tells the inhabitants, 'who have built your town on a rock. The crows ordinarily shit on the people, whilst you shit on the crows.'

The populous streets are more restless than those of Algiers, teeming with life, ceaselessly crossed by the most diverse beings, by Arabs, Kabyles, Biskris, Mzabis, Negroes, veiled Moorish women, spahis in red, *turcos* in blue, serious *kadis*, and resplendent officers.[4] And then there are merchants pushing in front of them asses—little African donkeys no taller than dogs— or horses, or slow and majestic camels.

Hello! to the Jewish women. Here they have a superb beauty, severe and charming. They pass by draped, rather than dressed; draped in bright fabrics, with an incomparable knowledge of the effects and nuances required to make them beautiful. They go about, their arms bare from the shoulder, the arms of statues that they boldly expose to the sun, and with their calm faces with pure and straight lines. And the sun seems powerless to bite into this sleek flesh.

But the gaiety of Constantine is the multitude of little girls, the very little girls. Fitted out as if for a costume party, clothed in trailing dresses of blue or red silk, wearing on their heads long gold or silver veils, with painted eyebrows lengthened into an arc above their eyes, tinted nails, the cheeks and forehead sometimes tattooed with a star, the gaze bold and already provocative, attentive to admiration, they trot along, giving their hand to some big Arab, their servant.

It's like a nation out of some fairy tale, a nation of little gallant women; for they have the air of women, these young girls, women in their toilette, in their already awakened coquetry, in the affectations of their faces. They catch your eye just as the older ones do; they are charming, worrying and irritating like adorable monsters. Like a boarding school of ten-year-old courtesans, in whom the seed of love has just blossomed.

Now here in front of us is the palace of Hadj-Ahmed, said to be one of the most complete specimens of Arabic architecture. All the travellers have celebrated it, comparing it to the dwellings from *The Thousand and One Nights*.

There would be nothing remarkable about it if the interior gardens didn't give it such a pretty oriental character. A whole volume would be needed to recount the ferocities, the misappropriations, and all the infamies of the one who built it with precious materials removed and torn out from the rich dwellings in the town and its surroundings.[5]

Constantine

The Arab part of Constantine forms half of the city. The streets slope, and are more jumbled and narrow than those of Algiers, running as far as the chasm where the Oued-Roumel flows.

Eight bridges formerly crossed this precipice. Six of these bridges are today in ruins. Only one, of Roman origin, gives us an idea of what it was like. The Roumel, from place to place, disappears under colossal arches, which it has carved out itself. On one of these the bridge was built. The natural vault through which the river runs is forty-one metres high, and eighteen metres thick; the foundations of the Roman construction are therefore *fifty-nine* metres above the water; and the bridge itself has two levels, two rows of arches superimposed upon the giant arch of nature.

Today an iron bridge, of one arch, provides the entrance into Constantine.[6]

But it is time to leave and make for Bône, a pretty white town reminiscent of those on the Mediterranean coast of France.

The *Kléber*[7] is heating up alongside the quay. It's six o' clock. When the steamer begins to move the sun is sinking over there, behind the desert.

And I stay until nightfall on the bridge, eyes turned towards the land which is disappearing in a crimson cloud, in the apotheosis of a sunset, in an ash of golden pink sown upon the great blue mantle of the tranquil sky.

Fragments

At the Spas [Aux Eaux]

THE DIARY OF THE MARQUIS DE ROSEVEYRE

***

12 June 1880.— To Loëche![1] They want me to spend a month in Loëche! Goodness gracious! One month in this town which is said to be the saddest, most dead, most boring of all spa towns! Did I say a town? It's a hole, barely even a village! I've been condemned to a month of penal servitude, well! well!

*13 June.—*I spent all night thinking about this trip which terrorizes me. There's only one thing left for me to do, I'm going to take a woman! Perhaps that will be able to distract me? And then from this experience I will learn if I am ripe for marriage.

A month long tête-à-tête, a month of living with someone, life as a couple, talks at any time of day or night.—Damn!

Taking a woman for a month, it's true, isn't as grave as taking her for life; but it's already a lot more serious than taking her for a night. I know that I can always send her back, with a few hundred louis;[2] but then I'll be on my own in Loëche, and that's not funny!

It will be a difficult choice. I don't want a flirt or a fool. I cannot be ridiculed by or ashamed of her. I'd really like to hear them say, 'How lucky is the marquis de Roseveyre'; but I don't want them whispering behind my back, 'Oh, the poor marquis de Roseveyre!' All things considered, I want my temporary companion to have all the qualities I expect of my definitive companion. The only difference will be that between something new and something second-hand. Oh well! it can be found, if I think about it!

Fragments

14 June.—Berthe! . . . That's my ticket. Twenty, pretty, just left the Conservatoire,³ awaiting a role, a future star. She's well mannered, proud, witty and. . .loving. The second-hand can pass for new.

15 June.—She is free. Without any commitments to any business or to any heart, she accepts, I order her dresses myself, so she won't look like a whore.

20 June.—Basle. She sleeps. I'm going to begin my travel notes.
She is completely charming. When she appeared in front of me at the station, I didn't recognize her, so much did she have the air of a woman of the world. She has a future, for sure, does this child. . .in the theatre.

She seems to me to have changed her manners, her gait, her attitude, her gestures, her smile, her voice, everything, and now she's irreproachable. And the way she was turned out! Oh! she was turned out in such a divine way, in the charming and simple way of a woman who no longer has to attract everyone's attention, no longer has to please everybody, whose role is no longer to seduce at first glance those who view her, but who wants to please discreetly and uniquely just one person. And that was shown in her entire mien. It was indicated so expertly and completely, the metamorphosis appeared to me so absolute and knowing, that I offered her my arm as I would have done to my wife. And she took it with ease, as if she had been my wife.

One on one in the brougham,⁴ we stayed motionless and mute at first. Then she raised her veil and smiled. . . Nothing more. A tasteful smile. Oh! I was fearful of the kiss, the comedy of tenderness, the eternal and banal games of girls; but no, she contained herself. She is strong.

Then we chatted, a bit like newly-weds, a bit like strangers. It was nice. She often smiled whilst looking at me. Now it was me who wanted to kiss her. But I remained calm.

At the border a braided official brusquely opened the door and asked me:
'Your name, Sir?'
I was surprised. I replied:
'Marquis de Roseveyre.'
'Where are you going?'
'To the spas of Loëche, in Valais.'⁵

At the Spas

He wrote something in a register. He resumed:

'Madame is your wife?'

What do I do? What do I answer? Hesitating, I looked at her. She was pale and staring into the distance. . . Either way, I felt that I was going to insult her needlessly. And then afterwards she was going to be my companion, for a month.

'Yes, Sir,' I pronounced.

I saw her blush. I was fortunate.

On arriving here at the hotel, the proprietor handed her the register. She straightaway passed it to me; and I knew that she was watching me write. It was our first night of intimacy! . . .Once this page was turned, who would read this register? I wrote out: 'Marquis and marquise de Roseveyre, going to Loëche.'

21 June.—Six o' clock in the morning. Basle. We leave for Berne. I definitely have the lucky touch.

21 June.—Ten o' clock in the evening. A strange day. I'm actually a little moved. It's stupid and funny.

During the trip we spoke little; she got up too early; she was tired; she dozed.

As soon as we were at Berne, we wanted to behold the panorama of the Alps which I had never seen; and we went across the town like a young married couple.

All of a sudden we were looking upon a limitless plain, and over there, down there, glaciers. From afar, like that, they don't seem that immense, but nevertheless this view gave me a frisson in my veins. A radiant setting sun was falling on us; the heat was terrible. But those white mountains of ice remain cold. The Jungfrau, la Vierge,[6] overlooking her brothers, stretching out her snowy flank; and standing everywhere about her, as far as the eye could see, pale-crowned giants, with their eternally frozen summits that the dying day made so bright, silver-plated in the dark blue of the evening.

This inert and colossal crowd gave the impression of the beginning of a new and surprising world, a precipitous, dead, fixed region, but with an attraction like the sea, full of the power of a mysterious seduction. The air which had always caressed these frozen summits seemed to come to us from over narrow and flowered countryside, different to the fecund air of the plains. It had something harsh and strong, something sterile about it, like the taste of inaccessible spaces.

Berthe, bewildered, looked out, speechless.

Suddenly she took my hand and squeezed it. I, myself, had this sort of fever in my heart, this exaltation which seizes us in the face of certain unexpected spectacles. I took this little, trembling hand and raised it to my lips; and I kissed it, indeed, with love.

I remained a little disturbed. But by what? By her, or by the glaciers?

24 June.—Loëche, ten o' clock in the evening.

The whole journey was delicious. We spent half the day in Thun,[7] looking at the rough frontier of mountains that we had to cross the following day.

Under the rising sun we crossed the lake, the most beautiful in Switzerland, perhaps. Some mules awaited us. Seated upon their backs, we departed. After lunching in a small town, we began the ascent, slowly entering the rising wooded gorge, always overlooked by high summits. Here and there on the slopes which seemed to come down from the sky, you could see white specks, chalets, built there one knows not how. We cleared torrents, and sometimes noticed, between two slender summits covered in fir trees, an immense pyramid of snow which seemed so close that you'd swear you could reach it in twenty minutes, but which in actual fact would take you twenty-four hours to reach.

Sometimes we crossed a chaos of stones, narrow plains strewn with caved in rocks, as if two mountains had bumped into each other in these lists, leaving on the battle field the debris from their granite limbs.

Berthe, exhausted, slept on her beast, opening her eyes every now and then. She ended up dozing off and I supported her with my hand, glad of this contact, of feeling through her dress the gentle heat of her body. Night came, we were still climbing. We stopped in front of a little inn concealed in the mountains.

We slept! Oh my, how we slept!

As day was breaking I ran over to the window and I gasped. Berthe came up beside me and remained stupefied and enraptured. It had snowed as we slept.

All about us the grey bones of enormous, barren mountains were jutting out beneath a mantle of white; mountains without pine trees, dull and frozen, rose so high they seemed inaccessible.

An hour after we had set off again, we noticed at the bottom of this hollow of granite and snow, a dark, black unstirring lake that we followed for quite a while.

At the Spas

A guide brought us some edelweiss, the pale flowers that grow on the glaciers. Berthe made a corsage out of them.

Suddenly, the gorge of rocks opened out in front of us, uncovering an astonishing horizon: the whole range of the Piedmontese Alps beyond the Rhône valley.

Great summits, here and there, overlooked the crowd of lesser peaks. They were Mont Rose, serious and weighty; le Cervin, the upright pyramid where so many men have died; la Dent-du-Midi;[8] and a hundred other white points gleaming like diamonds in the sun.

The path that we were following abruptly stopped at the edge of an abyss, and in this chasm, at the bottom of this black hole two thousand metres deep, enclosed between four walls of sheer, brown, savage rocks, on a lawn bed, we spotted a few white dots that looked like sheep in a meadow. They were the houses of Loëche.

We had to leave the mules, the road was too dangerous. The path snaked down the length of the rock, turning, coming and going, always overlooking the precipice, and the village too, which grew bigger as we got nearer. This is what is known as the Gemmi pass, one of the most beautiful in the Alps, if not the most beautiful.[9]

Berthe, leaning on me, let forth joyful, fearful cries, happy and scared like a child. As we were a few paces from the guides and hidden by a protrusion in the rock, she kissed me. I clasped her to me...

I had said to myself:

'At Loëche, I will have to take care to make it known that I am not with my wife.'

But so far I had treated her as such everywhere, and everywhere I had made her pass for the marquise de Roseveyre. I could hardly now register her under another name. If I did so I would wound her heart and she really was so charming.

But I said to her:

'My dear friend, you bear my name: they will believe me to be your husband; I hope that you will behave towards everyone with great prudence and the utmost of discretion. No acquaintances, no chats, no relations. They might believe you to be haughty, but at least you will be acting in a way that won't lead me to regret what I have done.'

She replied:

'You needn't worry, my little René.'

26 June.—Loëche isn't dreary. No. It's wild, but very beautiful. There is this rock wall two thousand metres high from which flow hundreds of mountain streams, like silver wires; an eternal noise of running water. This village is buried in the Alps from where one sees it as though at the bottom of a well, whilst the distant sun crosses the sky. Then there's the neighbouring glacier, completely white in the indentation of the mountain, and this valley full of streams, full of trees, full of freshness and life, which descends towards the Rhône, and lets you see the snowy peaks of Piedmont in the horizon: it all seduced and enchanted me. Perhaps because . . .if Berthe wasn't there?. . .

She is perfect, this child, more reserved and distinguished than anyone. I hear it said:

'How pretty she is, this little marquise!. . .'

27 June.—First bath. You go directly down to the pool, where twenty bathers soak, already clothed in long woollen robes, men and women together. Some eating, some reading, others chatting. Little floating tables are put in front of you. Sometimes you play hunt-the-slipper, which is not always appropriate. Seen from the galleries that surround the bath, we look like fat toads in a bucket.

Berthe came and sat down in this gallery to chat with me a bit. She was looked at a lot.

28 June.—Second bath. Four hours in the water. In eight days I will have to spend eight hours in the water. I have as fellow divers, the prince de Vanoris (Italy), the comte Lovenberg (Austria), the baron Samuel Vernhe (Hungary or somewhere), plus about fifteen people of less importance, but still all of nobility. Everyone is from the nobility in these spa towns.

They ask me, one after the other, to be introduced to Berthe. 'Yes yes!' I reply and I slip away. They think I am jealous, how stupid!

29 June.—Damn! Damn! Just as we were returning to the hotel, the princesse de Vanoris herself came to find me, wishing to make the acquaintance of my wife.

At the Spas

I introduced Berthe, but I beseeched her to take care to avoid running into this lady.

2 July.—The prince collared us yesterday and led us to his apartment, where all the bathers of distinction take tea. Berthe was, for sure, better than all the other women; but what can you do?

3 July.—So what, who cares! Among these thirty gentlemen, aren't at least ten of them fictional?[10] And out of the sixteen or seventeen wives, are more than twelve really married? And of those twelve, are any more than six of them irreproachable? Who cares, so much the worse for them! It's what they wanted!

10 July.—Berthe is the queen of Loëche! Everyone is crazy about her; they fête her, they spoil her, they adore her! What's more, she is superbly graceful and full of refinement. They envy me.
The princesse de Vanoris asked me:
'Ah! So, marquis, where did you find that treasure?'
I wanted to answer:
'She won first prize from the Conservatoire, in the comedy class, she is contracted to the Odéon,[11] but free to leave from *5 August 1880!*'
Goodness gracious, what a face she would have made!

20 July.—Berthe really is astonishing. Not one error in tact or taste; a real wonder!

***

10 August.—Paris. It's over. I have a heavy heart. The day before our departure I thought that everyone was going to cry.
It was resolved to go and watch the sun rise on the Torrenthorn,[12] then to come back down in time for our hour of departure.
We set off towards midnight, on mules. The guides carried lanterns; and the long caravan unwound in the twisting paths of the pine forest. Next we crossed pastures where herds of cows wandered freely. Then we reached the stony region, where the grass disappeared.

Sometimes, in the shadows, you saw either on the right, or on the left, a white mass, heaps of snow in the mountainside holes.

The cold became biting, stinging the eyes and the skin; the wind which was drying out the summits was blowing, burning our throats and carrying with it the frozen breaths of hundreds of leagues of icy peaks.

When we had, in fact, arrived, it was still night. We unpacked all the provisions in order to drink champagne as the sun was rising.

The sky was turning paler overhead. We had already noticed a chasm at our feet; then, a few hundred metres further on, another summit.

The entire horizon seemed to become pallid, but without us being able to distinguish anything more in the distance.

Soon, on the left, an enormous summit was uncovered—the Jungfrau—then another and another. They appeared little by little, as if they were rising up and forming themselves in time with the nascent day. And we remained astonished to find ourselves in the midst of these colossuses, in this desolate land of eternal snow. Suddenly, opposite us, the limitless chain of Piedmont was unfolding itself. Other summits appeared in the north. It really was a vast land of great, frozen-crowned mountains, from the Rhindenhorn, heavy like its name, as far as the ghostly, and barely visible patriarch of the Alps, Mont Blanc.[13] Some were standing upright and proud, others were squatting, others deformed, but all were similarly white, as if God had thrown some immaculate tablecloth over the uneven ground.

Some seemed close enough to jump on to; others were so distant that they could barely be made out.

The sky became red; and everything grew red. The clouds seemed to bleed upon everything. It was amazing, almost frightening.

But soon the enflamed skies paled, and the whole army of summits imperceptibly became pink, a soft and tender pink, like that of the dresses of a young girl.

And the sun appeared above the blanket of snow. Then, all of a sudden, the entire populace of glaciers was white, a shining white, as if the horizon had been full of a throng of silver domes.

Watching it all, the women were ecstatic.

They jumped, a champagne cork had just been popped; and the prince de Vanoris presented a glass to Berthe, exclaiming:

'A toast to the marquise de Roseveyre!'

Everyone shouted in response, 'to the marquise de Roseveyre!'

She got up on to her mule and replied:

'I toast to all my friends!'

Three hours later we were on the train for Geneva, in the Rhône valley.

Scarcely were we alone when Berthe, who had been so happy and gay all the time, began to sob, her face in her hands.

I fell at her knees:

'What's the matter? What's the matter? Tell me, what's the matter with you?'

She stammered through her tears:

'It's. . .it's. . .it's the end of being an honest woman!'

For sure, I was at this moment on the verge of committing a folly, a great folly!. . . I didn't do it.

I left Berthe on returning to Paris. I would, perhaps, have been too weak, later.

(The diary of the marquis de Roseveyre offers nothing of interest for the following two years. For the date marked 20 July 1883, we find the following lines.)

20 July 1883.—Florence. It's sad to remember sometimes. I was walking in the Cassines [14] when a woman stopped her carriage and called out to me. It was the princesse de Vanoris. As soon as she saw I was within range, she exclaimed:

'Oh! Marquis, my dear marquis, how happy I am to see you again! Quick, quick, tell me how the marquise is—truly the most charming woman I have seen in all my life.'

I was left dumbfounded, not knowing what to say, struck to the heart by a violent blow. I stammered:

'Never speak of her to me, princess, it's been three years since I lost her.'

She took my hand.

'Oh! How I pity you, my friend.'

She left me. I returned, sad, discontented, thinking of Berthe, as though we had just separated.

Destiny is very often mistaken!

Fragments

How many honest women were born to be prostitutes, and prove it.

Poor Berthe! How many others were born to be honest women. . .And she. . . more than any other. . .perhaps. . .Oh well. . .let's not think of it any more.

In Brittany [En Bretagne]

July 1882

This is the season of journeys, the bright season where one loves to have new horizons—the vast expanses of the blue sea—rest easy on the eye, the season where the spirit is calmed. Where sometimes the heart melts, you know not why, when you sit down as evening falls, in fresh wooded valleys upon the velvety green bank of a road, and when you notice at your feet, in the bottom of a rut dug out by the wheels of a cart, some dormant brown water in which the sun is reflected.

I am absurdly fond of walking in places that I have just discovered, where you find unexpected surprises owing to customs [*moeurs*] that you wouldn't have suspected, where your interest is constantly maintained, where your eyes can revel, provoking this endless awakening of thought.

One thing alone spoils these charming explorations for me: reading the guides. Written by commercial travellers in terms of kilometres, with odious descriptions that are always wrong, with invariably erroneous information and references to totally imaginary pathways, they are, with one exception—an excellent German guide—the consolation of hosiers on pleasure trips, visiting le *Joanne* country,[1] and they are the despair of true travellers who go about with their packs on their backs, cane in hand, along paths, ravines and beaches.

They lie, they know nothing, they contain nothing, they disfigure the most beautiful countryside with their stupid and emphatic prose; they know only the main roads and they are worth less than those Ordnance Survey maps[2] which are yet to mark out weirs on the Seine that were built thirty years ago.

Still, when travelling, how you love to know in advance a bit about the region in which you venture! And how lucky you are when you find a book in which some sincere vagabond has jotted down a few of his visions! Then it's not merely an introduction which prepares you only to know places. Sometimes it's more. When you sink deep into Algeria, as far as the oasis of Laghouat, each day, each hour of the journey you must read the admirable book by Fromentin, *Un Été dans le Sahara* [A Summer in the Sahara].[3] It opens your eyes and your spirit, and seems to throw more light on those plains, those mountains, those burning wildernesses, it shows you the soul of the desert.

Everywhere in France there are charming, almost unknown corners. Without claiming to make a new guide, I would like from time to time to mark out only a few short excursions, journeys of ten or fifteen days, accomplished by all the walkers, but ignored by all the sedentary people.

Never follow the main roads, always stick to the footpaths, sleep in barns when no inns are to be found, eat bread and drink water when other provisions are untraceable, and fear neither the rain, nor the distances, nor long hours of steady walking, that's what you have to do to traverse and penetrate into the heart of a region, in order to discover, so close to the towns where all the tourists stay, a thousand things you wouldn't suspect.

Out of all the old provinces of France, Brittany is one of the most curious; in ten days you can get to know enough to appreciate its temperament, for each region, like each man, has its own [temperament].

Let us pass through it in a few lines. Going only from Vannes to Douarnenez, following the coast, the true Breton coast, lonely and low, strewn with reefs, where the tide always roars and seems to be answered by the whistling of the wind across the moor.

The Morbihan, a kind of inland sea, which rises and falls according to the tides from the big Ocean, stretches out in front of the port of Vannes. You have to cross it to reach the broad one.

It is full of islands, mysterious, haunted, Druidic islands. They wear on their backs tumuli, menhirs, and dolmens, all these strange stones that were nearly gods.[4] According to the Bretons, these islets are as numerous as the days of the year. The Morbihan is a symbolic sea shaken by superstitions.

And that's the great charm of this region; it is the birthplace of legends. Dead

In Brittany

everywhere, the old beliefs remain entrenched in this granite soil. The old stories are also indestructible in this land; and the peasant speaks to you of adventures accomplished fifteen centuries before as if they happened yesterday, as if his father or grandfather had witnessed them.

There are underground passageways where the dead remain intact, like the day when they were struck down immobile, only dry, because the source of blood has dried up. And so memories live on forever in this corner of France, memories, and even the ancestors' ways of thinking.

I left Vannes the day of my arrival in order to go and visit an historic château, Sucinio,[5] and, from there, to go on to Locmariaker, then Carnac, and following the coast, Pont-l'Abbé, Penmarch, la pointe du Raz, and Douarnenez.

The path initially skirted the Morbihan, then went across a never-ending moor, interspersed with ditches full of water, and without a house, tree or being, only populated by a gorse that trembled and whistled in the furious wind which carried across the sky ragged clouds that seemed to moan.

Further on I crossed a little hamlet where three sordid peasants loitered barefoot with a buxom girl of twenty whose calves were blackened with manure; then again the moor, deserted, bare, and marshy as it goes to merge with the Ocean, whose grey line, sometimes highlighted by specks of foam, stretches out over there beyond the horizon.

And in the middle of this wild expanse, a tall ruin rose up; a square castle, flanked by towers, standing all alone between these two deserts: the moor and the sea.

The old manor of Sucinio, which dates from the thirteenth century, is illustrious. The great *connétable* de Richemont who took France back from the English was born there.[6]

There are no doors. I enter into the vast, isolated courtyard where the collapsed turrets have fallen into heaps of stones; and climbing what remains of the staircases, scaling broken walls, hanging on to ivy and pieces of half-loosened granite that came away in my hands, I reached the top of the tower, from where I could look over all Brittany.

Opposite me, behind a strip of uncultivated plain, the dirty Ocean, roaring under a black sky; then, everywhere, the moor! Over there on the right, the Morbihan sea with its torn up shores, and further on, barely visible, a white, illuminated patch, Vannes, lit up by a ray of sun that had somehow slipped between two clouds. Then still further on, an immeasurable cape: Quiberon!

Everything sad, melancholic and heart-rending. The wind cried as it passed through these desolate places; I really was in a haunted land; inside these walls, amongst the close-cropped and whistling gorse, in these ditches where water stagnates, I could feel the legends prowling.

The following day I crossed Saint-Gildas, where the ghost of Abélard seemed to wander.[7] At Port-Navalo, the sailor who took me across the strait talked to me about his father, a Chouan, of his elder brother, a Chouan, and his uncle, the priest, also a Chouan, all three of them dead. . .and he stretched out his hand, pointing out Quiberon.[8]

At Locmariaker I entered into the homeland of the Druids. A Breton showed me the table of Caesar[9]—a granite monster raised up by giants—then he spoke to me about Caesar as if of some old boy he might have seen.

Always following the coast, between the moor and the Ocean, towards evening, from the top of a tumulus, I finally spotted in front of me the fields of stones of Carnac.

They seemed like living things, these interminably aligned stones, giant or small, square, long, flat, looking like big, thin or paunchy bodies. When you look at them for a long time, you see them begin to stir, to lean, to live!

You lose yourself in the midst of them; sometimes a wall interrupts this granite crowd; you cross over it and the strange crowd starts up once more, spaced out like avenues, set out like soldiers, frightful like apparitions.

Your heart rules your head, your spirit becomes excited in spite of you, going back through the ages, losing itself in superstitious beliefs.

As I stayed motionless, amazed and delighted, a sudden noise behind me really made me jump and I turned round in a bound; and an old man dressed in black, with a book under his arm, having greeted me, said: 'Ah so, Sir, you are visiting our Carnac.' I told him how caught up in it all I'd been and the fright he'd given me. He continued: 'Here, Sir, there are so many legends in the air that everyone is scared without knowing why. Five years I've been digging under these stones; nearly all of them have a secret, and sometimes I even imagine that they have a soul. When I am back walking along the boulevards, I smile at my stupidity; but when I return to Carnac I am a believer, an unconscious believer; without any particular religion, but with something of all of them [religions].'

And, stamping his foot:

'This is a land of religion; one must never make light of extinct beliefs; for nothing dies. We are, Sir, in the home of the Druids, respect their faith!'

The sun, disappearing into the sea, had left the sky all red, and this light also bled upon the big stones neighbouring us.

The old man smiled.

'As you might imagine, these terrible beliefs have such power in this place that even right here I have had a vision! What am I saying! A veritable apparition! There, on that dolmen, one night, at about this time, I distinctly saw the enchantress Koridwen, who was boiling the miraculous water.'

I stopped him, not knowing who the enchantress Koridwen was.

He was outraged.

'What! You don't know the wife of the god Hu and the mother of *korrigans*!'

'I have to admit I don't. If it's a legend, please tell it to me.'

I sat down by his side on a menhir.

He began.

'The god Hu, father of the Druids, had the enchantress Koridwen for his wife. She gave him three children, Mor-Vrau, Creiz-Viou, a girl—the most beautiful in the world—and, Aravik-Du, the most frightful of all beings.

'Koridwen, in her maternal love, wanted to leave at least something to this son so ill favoured, and she resolved to make him drink the water of divination.

'This water had to be boiled for a whole year. The enchantress entrusted a blind man named Morda and a dwarf, Gwiou, to watch over the vase which contained the potion.

'The year was about to pass, when the two watchmen slackened in their zeal, and a little bit of the sacred drink was spilt, and three drops fell on to the finger of the dwarf, who raised it to his mouth, and suddenly knew the future. The vase shattered at once and Koridwen appeared, bearing down upon Gwiou, who fled.

'As he was about to be caught, he changed himself into a hare to run more quickly; but at once the enchantress became a greyhound and sprang behind him. She was going to seize him on the banks of a river, but he suddenly took the form of a fish and dashed away in the current. Then an enormous otter emerged which followed him so closely that he could only escape it by becoming a bird. However, a large sparrowhawk swooped down from the skies with outstretched wings and open beak; it was always Koridwen; and Gwiou, trembling with fear, changed himself into a grain of corn, letting himself fall on to a heap of wheat.

'Next, a big black hen ran up and swallowed it. Koridwen—avenged—rested, when she noticed that she was going to be a mother again.

'The grain of corn had germinated within her; and a child was born, one that Hu abandoned in a wicker cradle in the water. But the child, saved by the son of King Gouydno, became a genie, the sprite of the moor, the *korrigan*. And so all the little fantastic creatures—the dwarves, the elves that haunt these stones—are born of Koridwen. It's said they live below, in holes, and come out at night to run through the gorse. If you stay here long enough, Sir, amidst these enchanted monuments, watching fixedly some dolmen lying on the ground, you will soon hear the earth shiver, you will see the stone stir, you will tremble with fear, as you notice the head of a *korrigan*, looking at you as it lifts up the front of the block of granite placed above him. Now, let's go and have dinner.' [10]

Night had come, pitch-black and moonless, filled with murmuring wind. Hands outstretched, I walked, banging into the big, upright stones; and this story, this land, my thoughts, all had become so coloured by the supernatural, that I wouldn't have been surprised to suddenly feel a *korrigan* run between my legs.

The following day I continued on my way, crossing moors, villages, and towns. Lorient, Quimperlé, so pretty in its valley, and Quimper.

The main road leaving Quimper climbs a hill, cuts through valleys, passes a sort of grassy, desolate lake, and finally enters Pont-l'Abbé, the most Breton little city of all Breton-speaking Brittany, which stretches from the Morbihan to la pointe du Raz.

At the entrance an old castle flanked by towers wets the foot of its walls in a sad pond, [11] with flocks of wild birds. A river flows from there along which the coasters can sail as far as the town. [12] And in the narrow streets with their centuries-old houses, the men wear hats with huge brims, waistcoats embroidered magnificently and four jackets, one on top of each other: the first, as big as a hand, covers at most the shoulder blades, and the last stops just above the breeches' bottom.

The girls, tall, beautiful and fresh, have their bosoms compressed by cloth waistcoats which form a breastplate that clings to them, not even letting you guess at their powerful and martyred throats. And they wear their hair in a strange way. On the temples, two coloured, embroidered bands frame the face, tying back the falling hair in a cloth, which is then piled back on top of the head under a peculiar bonnet, often woven of gold or silver.

And the road leaves this small city of the Middle Ages behind, forgotten. It advances through the moor pricked with gorse. From time to time you see three or four cows grazing alongside the way, always accompanied by one sheep. For several days I had wondered why you never saw some cows without a sheep. This question worries you, badgers you, becomes an obsession. I looked for someone nearby who might be able to tell me. It's not easy to find anyone, for often you can stroll through these villages for an entire week without meeting anyone who knows a word of French. Finally there is a priest walking in measured strides as he reads his breviary, he politely informs you that this sheep constitutes the wolf's share.

A sheep is worth less than a cow and, as its capture offers no danger, the wolf always prefers to go for it. But it often happens that the valiant little cows form a square battalion to defend their innocent friend, and the howling beast, in its quest for living flesh, is met with the sharp ends of their horns.

The wolf! Here he is found, this legendary wolf that terrifies us in childhood, the white wolf, the great white wolf that all the hunters have seen, but none of whom have killed.

Never seen in the morning, it's towards five o' clock, in the winter, when the sun is going down, that it appears, ghosting along a bare hilltop, its long silhouette seen lingering against the sky as it passes and runs away.

Why has nobody killed him? Ah well! Here's a guess. The big hunting lunches always begin towards one o' clock and finish at four. A lot is drunk, and there is a lot of talk about the white wolf. When they leave the table, they see it. Is it really that surprising that they don't kill it?

I continued straight ahead on the grey road that was covered with granite which gleamed when the sun shone. On both sides the plain is flat, sown with gorse. Here and there a large lying stone keeps the memory of the Druids constantly in your thoughts; and the wind which blows low over the ground whistles in the thorny bushes. Sometimes a loud noise, like a distant cannon shot, makes the earth tremble; for I was nearing Penmarch, where the sea, so it's said, plunges deep into sonorous caverns. The waves, engulfed in these holes, shake the entire coast, making themselves heard as far as Quimper on stormy days.

Fragments

For a long time already I had noticed the great line of grey waves which seems to dominate the whole of this bare and low countryside. The waves breaking everywhere on rocks and on pointed reefs which show their black heads circled in froth as if they were drooling; and over there, against the water, a few chilly houses look to hide themselves behind little piles of stones trying to keep out of the eternal storm of the open sea and the salty rain of the Ocean. A big lighthouse, trembling on its platform of rocks, juts out into the waves, and the keepers say that sometimes on stormy nights, the long granite column pitches like a ship, and that the clock falls down, smashing its face on the floor, and that things attached to the walls detach, fall and break.[13]

From this place as far as Conquet, is the land of shipwrecks. It seems to be lying in wait for death, the hideous death of the sea: Drowning. There is no coast more dangerous or formidable, no coast more hungry for lives.

At the back of the low little houses of the fishermen, crawling in the mud with the pigs, you might see an old woman, or grown-up daughters with bare and dirty legs, or perhaps the sons, the oldest of whom is thirty at most. You almost never see the father or eldest son. Don't ask where they are, for the old woman will point to the rolling, rising horizon, which always seems ready to fling itself over this land.

It's not only the perfidious sea that devours these men. It has an all-powerful ally, yet more perfidious, to help it each night in its gluttonous feasting upon human flesh, and that is alcohol. The fishermen know it and admit it. 'When the bottle is full,' they say, 'you see the reef. But, when the bottle is empty, you no longer see it.'

The beach at Penmarch terrifies. It is here that shipwreckers used to attract lost vessels, by attaching to the horns of a cow—whose hoofs had been fettered to make it limp—a misleading lamp to simulate another ship.

Here, a little to the right, a rock became famous for a horrible drama. The wife of one of the last prefects of the Morbihan was sitting on this stone, with her little daughter on her lap. The sea, a few metres below them, seemed calm, inoffensive and dormant.

Suddenly one of those unusual waves that are called silent breakers[14] rose up and came without a noise; its back swollen, overwhelming, it scaled the rock, like a furtive malefactor, and it swallowed up and carried away the two women in an

In Brittany

instant. Some coastguards who were passing by in the distance only saw a pink parasol floating gently in the becalmed sea, and the big bare rock, streaming.

For a year the doctors and lawyers discussed, argued and pleaded in order to find out which of them, the mother or the child, carried away by the same wave, was killed first. They drowned cats with their littl'uns, dogs with their little doggies, rabbits with their young, so that no doubt remained, for the big question of the inheritance depended upon it, the fortune going to one or the other family according to whether the last convulsion had been in the body of the child or the grown-up. [15]

Almost opposite this sinister place stands a granite calvary, like those you see everywhere in this pious land where the crosses, themselves very old, are as numerous as their elder dolmens. But this calvary stood above a strange bas-relief, representing in a crude and comical way the childbirth of the Virgin Mary. An Englishman passing by admired the naïve sculpture and made a roof to cover it and to preserve it from the attacks of this wild climate. [16]

And so we follow the beach, the interminable beach all along la baie d'Audierne. You have to wade through or swim across two little rivers, and drudge through the sand or the seaweed, always going between these two wildernesses, the one moving, the other immobile, the sea and the moor.

Here is Audierne, a sad little port, animated only by the arrival and departure of boats going fishing for sardines.

Before leaving in the morning, instead of the everyday café au lait, you enjoy a few of these fresh fish sprinkled with salt—tasty, flavoursome, real violets of the waves. [17] And I head off towards la pointe du Raz, this end of the world, this tip of Europe.

You climb, you're always climbing, and suddenly you perceive two seas, on the left the [Atlantic] Ocean, and on the right the English Channel.

This is where they meet, where they fight unceasingly, their currents and their forever furious waves crashing into each other, capsizing ships and gobbling them down like sugar-coated almonds.

> *Ô flots, que vous savez de lugubres histoires,*
> *Flots profonds redoutés des mères à genoux.*

> [Oh the waves! I bet you know some gloomy stories,
> Deep waves ever dreaded by mothers on their knees.] [18]

Some more trees, then nothing but tufts of grass on the big headland which juts out. Right at the end, two lighthouses, and everywhere in the distance are other lighthouses, stuck into the reefs. One of them they have tried to complete for ten years. The sea, eager in pursuit, destroys the strenuous work of the men as soon as they accomplish it. [19]

Over there, opposite, is the île de Sein, the sacred island, looking out to the horizon, behind Brest harbour, at its dangerous crony, the île d'Ouessant.

> *Qui voit Ouessant*
> *Voit son sang,*

> [He who sees Ouessant
> Sees his own blood,]

say the sailors. [20] The île d'Ouessant, the most inaccessible of all, whom the sailors always approach in trembling.

The high promontory stops abruptly, a sheer fall into this battle of the oceans. But a little path skirts around it, crawling along the sloping granite, slipping along ridges no broader than a hand.

Suddenly you overlook a terrifying chasm, whose walls, as black as if they had been rubbed with ink, send back to you the furious din of the marine conflict delivering itself beneath you, at the bottom of this hole that they call l'Enfer [Hell]. [21]

Although I was a hundred metres above the sea, I was still sprayed by gobs of foam and, leaning over the abyss, I contemplated the fury of the water which seemed to have been provoked by an unknown rage.

It really was a hell that no poet had described. And a terror constrained me to thoughts of men thrown down there, rolled, turned and plunged into this storm between four stone walls, thrown against the mountain face, taken again by the waves, swallowed up, reappearing, bubbling about pell-mell in the monstrous waves.

And I set off once more on my way, haunted by these images, and battered by a strong wind which whipped this isolated headland.

In Brittany

After twenty minutes, I reached a little village. An old priest who was reading his breviary, sheltering behind a stone wall, greeted me. I asked him where I might be able to stay the night; he offered me his hospitality.

An hour later, both of us were sitting in front of his door, we were talking about this desolate land which captures the soul, when a little Breton, a child, passed barefoot in front of us, his long blond hair shaking in the wind.

The priest called to him in his mother tongue and the kid came over, all of a sudden becoming shy, eyes lowered and hands inert.

'He is going to recite his canticle for you,' said the priest, 'he's a sharp fellow gifted with a great memory and of whom I hope to make something.'

And the child began to mumble unknown words, in the whimpering tone of little girls who repeat their fables. He went along without full stops or commas, rolling out syllables as if the whole piece was formed of one word, only stopping for a second to inhale, then resuming his hurried whispering.

Suddenly he fell silent. It was finished. The priest gave him a little pat on the cheek.

'Very good, you can go.'

And the little scamp ran away. Then my host added:

'He has just told you an old canticle of this land here!'

I replied:

'An old canticle? Is it well known?'

'Oh! Not at all. I will translate it for you, if you like.'

And so the old man became animated, as if he were preaching, with a strong voice, raising his arms in a menacing gesture and inflating the words, declaiming this naïve and superb canticle, which I wanted to write down at his dictation.

Breton Canticle

Hell! Hell! Do you know what it is, sinners?

***

It is a furnace where the flames howl, and compared to it, a furnace like that which encloses the fire of a forge, or the fire that reddens the

Fragments

flagstones of an oven, they are nothing more than smoke!

***

You never see light there! The fire burns like a fever without being seen! Hope never enters there, because the anger of God has sealed the door!

***

There is fire above your heads, fire all around you! You are hungry? — Eat fire! — You are thirsty? — Drink from this river of sulphur and molten iron!

***

You will cry for eternity; your tears form a sea; and this sea will not be a drop of water for hell! Your tears will maintain the flames rather than extinguish them; and you will hear the marrow boiling in your bones.

***

Then your heads will be cut off above your shoulders, yet still you will live! Demons will fling them at each other, yet still you will live! They will roast your flesh on braziers; you will feel your flesh turning into coal; and yet still you will live.

***

And in hell there will still be other pains. You will hear reproaches, curses and blasphemies.

***

In Brittany

The father will say to his son: 'Be cursed, son of my flesh, it was for you that I wanted to amass goods through pillage!'

***

And the son will reply: 'Curses! Cursed be you, father; for it was you who gave me my pride and led me here.'

***

And the daughter will say to her mother: 'A thousand misfortunes on you, mother, a thousand misfortunes on you, cavern of impurities, for you left me to be free, and I left God!'

***

And the mother will not recognize her children any more; and she will reply:

***

'Curses upon my daughters and my sons, curses upon the sons of my daughters and the daughters of my sons!'

***

And these cries will resound for Eternity. And these sufferings will forever be. And this fire!. . .this fire!. . .it's the anger of God that lit it, this fire!. . .it will burn forever without languishing, without smoke, without penetrating your bones any less deeply.

***

Eternity!... Misfortune!... Never ceasing to die, never ceasing to drown in an ocean of sufferings!

Oh *never*! you are a word bigger than the sea! Oh *never*! you are full of cries and tears and rage. *Never*! Oh! you are severe. Oh! how you terrify!²²

And when the priest had finished, he said to me:
'Isn't that terrible?'
And down there we heard the tireless waves beating down unceasingly upon the sinister cliff. I could see once more that hole full of a furious foam, dismal, howling, a true place of death; and something of the mystical fear, which makes the repenting devotee tremble, weighed upon my heart.

I set off again as the sun was rising, reckoning to reach Douarnenez before nightfall.

A man who spoke French, having sailed fourteen years on navy ships, approached me as I was looking for the coastguard path, and we went down together towards la baie des Trépassés, of which la pointe du Raz forms one of the sides.

It's an immense amphitheatre of sand, of an unforgettable melancholy, a disturbing sadness which after a while makes you want to leave and move further on. A bare valley with a baleful pond, with no great amount of gorse, a pond which appears dead, ends up at this frightful shore.²³

It all seems like an antechamber to some infernal abode. The yellow sand, sad and flat, stretches out as far as an enormous granite headland which faces la pointe du Raz, and where the persistent waves break.

From a distance we noticed three motionless men stuck like piles in the sand. My companion appears astonished for no one ever comes into this desolate creek. But, on approaching, we saw something long stretched out near them, as though buried in the shore; sometimes they bent over and touched it, then straightened up.

It was a dead body, a drowning, a sailor from Douarnenez lost the previous week with four of his comrades. For eight days they had waited for them in this place where the current throws up the corpses. He was the first to arrive at this last rendez-vous.

But something else was preoccupying my guide, for drownings in this land are not rare. He took me towards the sad pond, and made me bend over the water,

In Brittany

and he pointed out to me the walls of the town of Ys. There were some ancient stoneworks, hardly visible. I went to drink from the spring, a very thin trickle of water, the best in the whole region, so it's said. Then he told me the history of this disappeared city, as if it was a still recent event, that had perhaps happened under the eyes of his grandfather.

A king, good but weak, had a depraved and beautiful daughter, so beautiful in fact that men were driven mad upon seeing her, so depraved that she gave herself to all of them, then had them killed, thrown into the sea from the top of the neighbouring rocks.

Her licentious passions were more violent, it was said, than the waves of the furious Ocean, and without doubt, harder to assuage. Her body seemed to be a hearth where hearts burned themselves before Satan then gathered them in.

God grew weary and he forewarned an old saint who lived in the land of his projects. The saint alerted the king, who didn't dare punish and lock up his cherished daughter, but he did inform her of God's warning. She paid it no heed and, on the contrary, gave herself up to such excesses that the whole town began to copy her, turning into a city of love, in which all decency and virtue had completely disappeared.

One night God woke up the saint to announce to him the hour of his vengeance. The saint ran to the king, who alone in this land had remained virtuous. The king made to saddle his horse, offering another to the saint, who accepted; a great din frightened them, and they saw that the sea was coming in over the countryside, jumping and bellowing. Then the king's daughter appeared at her window, screaming: 'Daddy, are you going to leave me to die?' And the king took her up behind him, then fled through one of the town gates just as the waves were entering by another.

They galloped through the night, but the waves continued to flow with terrible rumbles and downfalls. The rampant foam was already reaching the horses' feet, and the old saint said to the king: 'Sire, throw your daughter from your horse, or else you are lost.' And the daughter screamed: 'Daddy, daddy, don't abandon me!' But the saint drew himself up on his stirrups, his voice resounded like thunder and he announced: 'It is the will of God.' And so the king pushed back his daughter who was clinging to him, and she fell behind him. Immediately the waves seized her, then receded.

And the mournful pond which covers these ruins is the water that has since remained over the impure and destroyed town.

This legend is thus the story of Sodom rearranged for the instruction of women.

And the event spoken of as if it were yesterday, happened, it seems, in the fourth century after the coming of Christ. [24]

In the evening I reached Douarnenez.

It's a little fishing town which would be the most famous seaside resort in France if it was less isolated.

What gives it its charm and grace is its gulf. It is seated at the bottom and seems to look out at the long gentle line of hills, undulating, always rounded in charming curves, and whose distant peaks are drowned in those white and blue mists, so light and transparent, which the sea releases.

I set off again the following day for Quimper; and in the evening I sleep at Brest in order to take at daybreak the railway for Paris.

Le Creusot [1]

The sky is blue, very blue, and full of sunshine. The train has just passed Montchanin. [2] Over there, in front of us, a black, opaque cloud rises, seeming to rise straight out of the ground, obscuring the bright azure of the day, a heavy, motionless cloud. It's the smoke from [le] Creusot. As you get nearer, you can discern it. A hundred giant chimneys belching serpents of smoke into the air, smaller ones panting and spitting out vapour breaths; it all merges, spreads out and lingers, covering the town, filling the streets, hiding the sky, extinguishing the sun. It's almost dark now. A coal dust flies about, pricks the eyes, stains the skin, spatters the linen. The houses are black, like they've been rubbed in soot, the paving stones are black, the window panes are powdered with coal dust. The odour from the chimneys, of tar, of oil, floats in the air, contracting the throat, oppressing the chest, and sometimes there's the bitter taste of iron, of the forges, of burning metal, of burning hell, which stops you breathing and makes you raise your eyes in search of pure air, fresh air, the clean and healthy air of the great firmament; but instead, hovering above is the thick dark cloud, and flashing close by you, tiny facets of coal which fly about.

This is le Creusot.

A deafening and continuous noise makes the ground tremble, a noise made up of thousands of noises, a noise intermittently broken up by a tremendous blast, a shock that shakes the entire town.

We enter the factory of Messrs Schneider. [3]

What enchantment! This is the kingdom of Iron, where His Majesty Fire reigns!

The fire! you see it everywhere. Immense buildings aligned as far as the eye can see, as tall as mountains and full of different types of machine that turn, fall, rise up again, cross, shake, whirr, whistle, grate and shout. And all toiling with fire.

Here there are braziers, over there jets of flame, further on blocks of burning iron come and go, out of the furnaces and into the gearwheels, coming out and going back in again hundreds of times, changing shape, but always red. The voracious machines eat this fire, this glaring iron, they crush it, cut it, saw it, flatten it, spin it, twist it, make locomotives from it, ships, cannons, thousands of diverse things, some as fine as an artist's engravings, some like the monstrous works of giants, complicated things, delicate things, brutal things, powerful things.

Let's try to describe it, to understand it.

We enter on the right, under a vast gallery where four enormous machines work. They slowly turn their wheels, pistons and rods. What do they do? Nothing, except blow air into the tall furnaces where the molten metal boils. They are the monstrous lungs of the colossal retorts that we are going to see. They breathe, nothing else; they bring to life and assimilate the monsters.

And here are the retorts: there are two of them at either end of another gallery, big in girth, paunchy, roaring and spitting such jets of flame that your eyes are blinded and skin burnt from a hundred metres away, and you are made to pant like in a steam room.

You could compare it to a furious volcano. The fire which exits the mouth is white, unbearable on the eyes and projected with an indescribable force and noise.

Inside there the steel boils, Bessemer steel from which railways are made.[4] A strong, handsome, young and serious man capped in a big black felt hat, attentively watches this frightful blast. He is seated in front of a wheel similar to the wheel of a ship and sometimes he turns it in the same way as pilots do. Immediately the fury of the retort increases, it spits out a storm of flames, this is because the chief caster has just further increased the monstrous currant of air which runs through it.

And, still like a captain, the man constantly raises to his eyes a pair of binoculars to check the colour of the fire. He makes a gesture; a tip-truck advances and pours other metals into the raging brazier. The caster continues to observe the nuances in colour of the furious flames, looking for indications, then, suddenly turning another little wheel, he makes the formidable vat rock. It turns over slowly, spitting out a terrifying jet of sparks as high as the gallery ceiling; and it pours delicately, like an elephant striving to be graceful, a few drops of a blazing liquid into a smelting receptacle held out to it, then it redresses itself, roaring all the while.

A man carries this fire away. It is only now that a red ingot is placed under a steam-propelled hammer. The hammer strikes and crushes the burning metal, making it as thin as a sheet of paper, then it is immediately cooled in water. It is seized with a pair of tongs and broken; then the foreman examines the grain before giving the order: 'Pour it!'

The retort is immediately turned over anew and, like a servant filling up glasses around a table, it pours out a blazing cascade of steel which is carried away at the sides in a series of smelting receptacles placed round about it.

It seems to move in a natural way, very simply, as if it was a living being. In order to stir these fantastic engines, to get them to do their work, to get them going, to make them rise, fall, and redress themselves, to make them turn and pivot, all that's needed is to push levers no thicker than canes, to press buttons like those of electric doorbells. An energy, a strange spirit seems to look down upon them, to govern the weighty yet easy movements of these surprising devices.

We leave, faces roasted, eyes bloodshot.

Now we come across two brick towers in the open air, too tall to place under a roof. An unbearable heat is released from them. A man, armed with an iron lever, strikes them at the base, making a kind of coating fall away, then he digs more deeply. And soon a glimmer appears, a clear point. Two blows later and a stream, a torrent of fire bursts forth, running into channels dug in the ground, going, coming, always flowing. It's the cast iron, the molten pig iron. This frightful river takes your breath away, you flee, entering into tall buildings where locomotives, heavy machinery and battleships are made.

You can no longer make anything out, you don't know anything anymore, you lose your head. It's a labyrinth of moving cranks, wheels, belts and gears. At every step you find yourself in front of some monster working on iron, be it glowing red or dark. Here there are saws which divide up sheets of metal as wide as a body; over there pointed tools bore into blocks of cast iron, piercing them as easily as a needle does cloth; further on another machine cuts out strips of steel like a pair of scissors cutting a sheet of paper. Everything works at the same time, but with different movements, a fantastic population of disagreeable and rumbling beasts. And everywhere you see fire, under the hammers, in the furnaces, fire everywhere, and everywhere fire. And always a formidable and regular din dominates the tumult of wheels, boilers, anvils, mechanisms of all sorts, making the ground tremble. It is the big [ore-crushing] stamp of [le] Creusot at work.

It is at the end of a huge building which contains ten or twelve others. They all beat down periodically on an incandescent block, throwing up a shower of sparks, flattening it little by little, rolling it into a curved or straight or flat shape, according to the will of the men.

The big one weighs a hundred thousand kilos and it falls, bearing down like a mountain, upon a piece of red steel still bigger than itself. With each impact a storm of fire gushes out on all sides, and you can see the thickness of this mass that the monster works upon diminishing.

It rises and falls ceaselessly with a gracious facility, manipulated by a man who gently pulls upon a fragile lever; and it makes you think of those tales of bygone days which talk of terrifying animals being tamed by children.

We enter the gallery of the rolling mills. It is an even stranger spectacle. Red serpents running along the ground, some as thin as pieces of string, some as big as cables. Here they are like immeasurable earthworms, and there like frightful boas. For here iron wires are made, and there rails for trains.

Men, their eyes covered by wire gauze, their hands, arms and legs in leather, are forever throwing pieces of burning iron into the mouths of machines. The machine seizes it, pulls it, lengthens it, pulls it some more, releases it, takes it up again, always thinning it out. The iron twists around like a wounded snake, seeming to fight, but it yields, it is lengthened some more, always getting longer as it is released and taken up again by the steel jaws.

Here are the rails. Powerless to resist, the reddened, opaque and squared mass of Bessemer is stretched out by the efforts of the mechanics and, in a few seconds, becomes a rail. A gigantic saw cuts it down to its right length and others endlessly follow after it, nothing stops or slows down the formidable work.

Finally, we leave, we have ourselves become blackened like stokers, exhausted, our sight extinguished. And above our heads stretches out the thick cloud of carbon and the smoke which rises up to the heights of the sky.

Le Creusot

Oh! for some flowers, a meadow, a stream and some grass where you can lie down without thought and without another noise about you save the babbling of the water or the crow of a cock in the distance!

Notes
Appendix
Index

Notes

To the Sun

Chapter One

[1] Pol Arnault (or Arnauld) was one of Maupassant's Chatou (a town on the Seine, west of Paris, oft-frequented by Maupassant) boating friends.

[2] The quotation is from Gustave Flaubert, *A Sentimental Education*, tr. Douglas Parmée (Oxford: Oxford University Press, 2000), pt. 3, ch. 1, p. 351, where Flaubert is commenting on the palace of Fontainebleau:

> Royal residences have their own peculiar melancholy atmosphere which no doubt springs from the fact that they are far too large for the small number of people who live in them, from the surprising stillness which greets you after such an introductory blare of trumpets, and from their luxury, which has grown stiff with age and bears witness to the frailty of dynasties and the eternal wretchedness of all things.

The melancholy ennui Maupassant exhibits in this opening section of *To the Sun* mirrors his feelings of grief following the death of Flaubert on May 8, 1880, as shown in a letter to Flaubert's niece Caroline Commanville, May 24, 1880, where Maupassant also uses the same quotation from *A Sentimental Education*:

> *Je sens en ce moment d'une façon aiguë l'inutilité de vivre, la stérilité de tout effort, la hideuse monotonie des événements et des choses et cet isolement moral dans lequel nous vivons tous, mais dont je souffrais moins quand je pouvais causer avec lui; car il avait, comme personne, ce sens des philosophies qui ouvre sur tout*

des horizons, vous tient l'esprit aux grandes hauteurs d'où l'on contemple l'humanité entière, d'où l'on comprend l'« éternelle misère de tout ».

[At this moment I feel acutely the uselessness of living, the fruitlessness of trying, the hideous monotony of events and things, and the moral isolation in which we all live, but I suffered less when I chatted with him [Flaubert]; for he, like no other, had a great understanding of philosophy that opened up all horizons, taking your spirit to great heights from where the whole of humanity is contemplated, and where the 'eternal wretchedness of all things' is understood.—*Translations are mine unless stated otherwise*]

3   In 1881, before his trip to Algeria, Maupassant was living at 83 rue Dulong, in Paris. Maupassant was still living at the same address at the end of 1883 when this opening section of *To the Sun* was most probably written.

4   The opening stanza of 'Midi' ['Noon'], from *Les poèmes antiques* (1852), by the French poet Charles Marie Rene Leconte de Lisle (1818-94). Leconte de Lisle, born in La Réunion in the Caribbean, moved to Paris in 1845 to ply his trade as a poet and his works include *Poèmes barbares* (1862) and *Poèmes tragiques* (1884). He was a keen supporter of the abolition of slavery and the leader of the Parnassian movement. He was elected to the French Academy in 1886.

5   Madame Antoinette Deshoulières (née Du Ligier de la Garde, 1638-94), French poet who became the first female member of a French Academy, the Académie d'Arles, in 1689. Author of *Poésies* (1688). Maupassant is most probably alluding to her 1693 poem 'Allégorie' (no. 167 of *The Oxford Book of French Verse*, 1920) with the lines:

Dans ces prés fleuris
Qu'arrose la Seine,
Cherchez qui vous mène,
Mes chères brebis.

[In these flowered meadows
  That the Seine waters,
  Look for who leads you,
  My dear flock.]

6   Cheikh Mohammed ben Arbi-Hadji Bou-Amama (1833-1908), led the rebellion

of the Sud-Oranais nomads. See my 'Introduction', pp. x-xi, and ch. V of *To the Sun*, for more.

⁷ Gustave Flaubert (1821-80), left Paris on October 29, 1849 to tour Egypt, Palestine, Syria, Turkey, Greece and Italy. For further information see Gustave Flaubert, *Flaubert in Egypt*, tr. and ed. Francis Steegmuller (Harmondsworth: Penguin, 1996).

Chapter Two: The Sea

¹ Maupassant uses the Provençal phrase *troun de l'air*, an expression which can refer to a lively, playful woman, or alternatively it can stand for a particularly unbearable child. *Tron* or *troun* can also, more simply, be a synonym for 'thunder'.

² Maupassant uses another Provençal word, *pécaïre*, a compassionate interjection of commiseration meaning 'poor'.

³ Construction on le bassin de la Joliette commenced in 1844 as part of the enlargement of the port of Marseille, it was inaugurated in 1853 and remodelled in 1930.

⁴ Built in 1880, the *Abd El Kader* was the eighth of a series of twelve iron paquebots, serving the Compagnie Générale Transatlantique on the Marseille-North Africa line until it was demolished in 1922.

⁵ The first electric telegraph lines in Algeria were installed in 1854 replacing the semaphore system devised by Claude Chappe (1763-1805) which had been used by the military up until then. There were some protestations over the electric telegraph with fears that the wires could be cut.

⁶ In French, '*inspecteur général des ponts-et-chaussées*', lit. 'an inspector general of bridges and roads'. The *Corps des ponts et chaussées*, a state body dealing with travel infrastructure and civil engineering, was established in 1716 with one *inspecteur général*. The *Corps* developed and expanded with the founding of *l'École des ponts et chaussées* in Paris in 1747, the number of *inspecteurs généraux* likewise increasing.

⁷ Albert Grévy (1829-99) was acting Governor-General of Algeria from March 1879 to November 1881.

Chapter Three: Algiers

¹ Tartarin is a Don Quixote-style character from the Midi created by Alphonse Daudet (1840-97) in *Tatarin de Tarascon* (1871) and the sequels *Tartarin sur les Alpes* (1886) and *Port Tarasco* (1890). Daudet describes 'les Teurs' in *Tartarin de Tarascon* (Paris:

Ernest Flammarion, 1919), pt. 1, ch. XIII, p. 30:

> Pour Tarascon, l'Algérie, l'Afrique, la Grèce, la Perse, la Turquie, la Mésopotamie, tout cela forme un grand pays très vague, presque mythologique, et cela s'appelle les Teurs (les Turcs).

> [For in Tarascon, Algeria, Africa, Greece, Persia, Turkey and Mesopotamia all formed a big, very vague and almost mythological country called les Teurs (the Turks).]

[2] A sou is an old French copper coin worth, after the introduction of decimal currency in 1795, $1/_{20}$ of a franc and equivalent to five centimes. A sou would more generally be used to describe a small or trifling amount of money.

[3] *Arbico* means 'little arab'.

[4] Charles Louis Napoleon Bonaparte (1808-73) was President of the French Republic (1848-51), before seizing control of government on December 2, 1851, after a coup d'état. A year later he became Emperor of France (1852-70).

[5] Mustapha is an area of Algiers.

[6] La fête de Neuilly, also known as la fête à Neu-Neu, is an annual fair that takes place in Paris near the Bois de Boulogne; in Maupassant's day it would usually last three weeks or so in June-July with stalls and attractions stretching from Porte Maillot to the pont de Courbevoie.

[7] Maupassant uses the suitably obscure compound *femmes-silures* [lit. 'catfish-women']. Fake mermaids were often popular sideshow exhibits at nineteenth-century carnivals, ranging from actresses posing as mermaids to optical illusions presenting the living 'Girl in the Fish Bowl' to such hoaxes as the Feejee Mermaid, exhibited by P T Barnum (1810-91) in New York in 1842, which was made of the head of an ape woven on to the body of a fish.

[8] The Bal Bullier was a dancehall built by François Bullier (1796-1869) in 1843 near the Observatoire in Paris. It was mainly frequented by students.

[9] *Chahuts* are lively dances in the manner of cancans.

Chapter Four: The Province of Oran

[1] By the decree of April 24, 1845, Algeria was divided into three provinces: Oran, Algiers, and Constantine. A decree of December 9, 1848, gave the civil territories of

Notes

the three provinces the status of départements. A decree of October 24, 1870 united the civil and military territories.

2   The plain of Mitidja is to the south and south-west of Algiers. Kabylie is a mountainous area in north-eastern Algeria along the coast between Algiers and Bejaïa [Bougie]. Stretching about 125 km inland from the coast, it is an isolated, wild, but green area where the Berber people speak the Kabyle dialect, not Arabic.

3   Pas-de-Calais is a French département (no. 62) on the coast of the English Channel.

4   A marabout is a spiritual leader in Islam, it comes from the Berber word meaning 'hermit' or 'saint'; it may also refer, as here, to the tomb of a marabout or a shrine to his memory.

5   A burnous is a long hooded, woollen cloak-like garment worn in one piece.

6   *Douars* are gatherings of tents arranged in circles.

7   Nanterre, the capital of the Hauts-de-Seine département (no. 92), is a town on the western outskirts of Paris, situated on the river Seine. Rueil-Malmaison is found just to the south of Nanterre.

8   Stretching more than 600 km eastward from the Moroccan border, the hauts plateaux consist of undulating, steppe-like plains lying between the Tell and Saharan Atlas mountain ranges.

9   Mountain range stretching 2,400 km from the Atlantic coast of Morocco in the west to the Gulf of Gabès in Tunisia to the east; and found between the Mediterranean on the north and the Sahara to the south.

10 The Habra dam was built between 1865 and 1871. On December 15, 1881 part of the dam collapsed and 250 people were drowned and houses and bridges destroyed. The dam was rebuilt with modifications between 1883-5 at a cost of 1, 300, 000 francs. On March 12, 1879 there were floods in Hungary, when the river Tisza flooded the city of Szeged, killing 160 and making 60,000 homeless; and on October 15, 1879 in Murcia in Spain, the Segura basin experienced a flash flood (the 'Santa Teresa' flood) with 761 killed.

11 Abd-el-Kader ben Mahi-el-Dîn (1807 or 1808-1883), Algerian military and political leader, Islamic scholar, mystic, author and figurehead of Algerian independence. After the French conquest of Algiers, the tribes of Oran elected him as emir and he led a lengthy struggle against the French (1832-47). After his surrender to the French in 1847, Abd-el-Kader was exiled to France, although he was released by Napoléon III in 1855 on condition that he didn't return to Algeria. He devoted himself to theology

and philosophy, writing the book *Rappel à l'intelligent, avis à l'indifférent* (1858), a philosophical encyclopedia, as well as poetry and a study on Arab horses. In 1860 the French government awarded him the Grand Cross of the Légion d'honneur for his role in saving many lives when the Islamic Druze sect began to massacre Maronite Christians in Damascus. Abd-el-Kader made Saïda his stronghold in 1830 but he burnt it down in 1841 when he realized it couldn't be protected from French attack. The ruins of the fort can be found on the precipice known as Vieux Saïda.

[12] An *oued* or 'wadi' in English, is a valley or riverbed that remains dry except during the rainy season.

[13] In the French, '*la haute négresse. . .qui laisse sur son passage un fumet de chair humaine à tourner les coeurs les plus solides*', which I have translated rather literally. The French phrase *tourner le cœur* can mean 'to turn one's stomach', 'feel ill' and one could possibly translate Maupassant's words as 'leaving behind in her wake a body odour that would make the strongest of stomachs heave'. But *tourner les coeurs* can be used amorously and sensually, 'a girl who turns heads'; and also morally 'turning hearts towards God', indeed '*tourner les coeurs des pères vers les enfants*' is used in some French translations of Luke 1.17, 'to turn the hearts of the fathers to the children' (Authorized Version). I don't think Maupassant is using the phrase in connection with love, spirituality or morality. He could be using it in disgust. But he could also be using it with an element of troubled sensuality, if we compare it back to the bare, disconcerting ankles of the veiled woman in ch. III (p. 11).

[14] After the Franco-Prussian War of 1870-1, in which Prussian troops advanced into France, defeating the French at Sedan, numerous people from Alsace and Lorraine who refused German rule emigrated to Algeria.

[15] The beys of Tunis had borrowed heavily in the mid-nineteenth century in an attempt to modernize their country only to end up going bankrupt. In 1869 Britain, Italy and France were put in control of Tunisian finance. In 1878 Britain and France came to a secret agreement that Britain would let France have control of Tunisia if France recognized Britain's presence in Cyprus. On the excuse of Tunisian tribesman crossing the Algerian border, France made a pre-emptive strike ahead of Italy and sent an army into Tunisia. The Bey of Tunis, Muhammad III as-Sadiq (1813-82; r. 1859-81) came to agreement with France and Tunisia was formerly declared a French protectorate by the Treaty of Bardo, May 12, 1881.

[16] The Tell is the name given to the region stretching along the Mediterranean coast,

it is where almost all of Algeria's arable land is found, and also where the vast majority of Algerians live, enjoying warm summers and rainy winters. It is bounded to the south by the Tell Atlas mountains.

[17] Chott is the Arabic word for a salt lake, of which there are many dotted along the hauts plateaux.

[18] The sirocco is a hot, dry and dusty wind that blows from the highlands of Africa towards the Mediterranean.

[19] The Compagnie Franco-Algérienne was given the exclusive privilege of cultivating esparto over an area of 300, 000 hectares in return for their building of the Arzew to Saïda railway line which opened in 1879. Esparto is a greyish-green grass that grows to over a metre in height. Native to Iberia, *Stipa tenacissima*, is widely grown in sandy places across the globe, the leaves being used for the manufacture of paper, rope, baskets, mats, etc.

[20] Different reports have given different figures for the Spanish casualties at the hands of Bou-Amama's forces, one report says 191 were killed or missing with 322 suffering material losses, another report says 134 killed or missing and 163 suffering material losses, for more see Jean-Jacques Jordi, *Espagnol en Oranie: histoire d'une migration 1830-1914* (Nice: Éditions Jacques Gandini, 1996), the statistics are from pp. 146-7. See also ch. V of *To the Sun* for Maupassant's account of the massacres.

[21] i.e., the little bustard (*otis tetrax*).

[22] The Zouaves are the corps of French infantry soldiers first raised in Algeria in 1831 from the Berber Kabyle people of the Zouaves, characterized by colourful oriental uniforms and precision drilling.

[23] Horsemen from a *goum*, a military contingent supplied by a tribe to the French army.

Chapter Five: Bou-Amama

[1] Muslim spiritual leader.

[2] Lieutenant Weinbrenner was 2nd in command of the *bureau arabe* of Géryville. He was charged with the task of arresting Taïeb and Merzouk, two emissaries of Bou-Amama. Weinbrenner and one of his accompanying spahis were killed on April 21, 1881, in the village of Oudeï-El-Hadjel amongst the Djeramna tribe, after having demanded the surrender of the emissaries. One of the spahis escaped immediately, the other two got away after being held captive for six days.

Notes

³ A *caïd* is an Arab tribal chief.

⁴ Joseph Charles Alexis Alfred Innocenti (1824-93). Colonel of the 4th chasseurs d'Afrique, Innocenti was made a general in January 1883.

⁵ An agha, or aga, from the Turkish word for 'lord', is a title of nobility, applied to military commanders in the Ottoman Empire, but in general to men of high standing; an agha is superior to a *caïd*. Aghas were appointed by the French Minister of War on recommendation of commandants of sub-divisions (of the three provinces).

⁶ The Chellala incident took place at about 8.30 a.m. on May 19, 1881. Official views of the skirmish differed greatly from those that appeared in some sections of the press. What Innocenti, the President of the Republic, and the Minister of War painted as a victory, was derided as a devastating defeat by some newspapers, who were particularly critical of Innocenti and his arrangement and manoeuvring of his troops. The cloudiness surrounding the incident is perhaps best illustrated by the varying casualty figures given. Innocenti, in his *Insurrection du Sud-Oranais en 1881: Bou-Amema et le Colonel Innocenti* (Paris: Téqui, 1893), says that 300 rebels were killed and 700 injured; 37 of his column were killed, with 16 injured, and 15 deserters. Capitaine Armengaud, in his *Le Sud Oranais: Journal d'un Légionnaire* (Paris and Limoges: Henri Charles-Lavauzelle, 1893), says that 300 rebels were killed, with 72 of Innocenti's troops killed, 13 injured, 12 deserters, and the loss of part of the convoy of provisions and baggages. Le Commandant E Graulle, in *Insurrection de Bou-Amama (Avril 1881)* (Paris: Henri Charles-Lavauzelle, 1905), says that 200 were killed on Bou-Amama's side, with Inocenti suffering the loss of 60 men killed and 22 injured.

⁷ Jean-Baptiste Cérez (1820-89). French general who was in command of the Oran division at the time of Bou-Amama's rebellion.

⁸ That is Sarraoui or Sahraoui, agha of the Harrars. Possibly the Agha El Hadj Kaddour ben Sahraoui who was awarded the Grand Cross of the Légion d'honneur in 1930.

⁹ Paul-Alexandre Detrie (1828-99). French general. Commander of the Légion d'honneur, Detrie commanded a sub-division of Dellys and, later, Oran.

¹⁰ Colonel Mallaret was head of the French Foreign legion from 1870-81.

¹¹ Possibly Sidi Cheikh Haj Tayyeb (d. 1935).

Chapter Six: The Province of Algiers

¹ Maupassant is referring to people from Algiers, rather than Algerians in general. The citizens of Algiers would later come to be described as *Algérois*. Maupassant also

Notes

seems to use the word *Algériens* with some sense of meaning colonists, and perhaps in this instance with particular emphasis on those *colons* who have been born and grown up in the city (or province) of Algiers.

2 Spahis are soldiers from the indigenous cavalry corps of the French army in Algeria.

3 The *bureaux arabes* were an administrative structure established at the beginning of colonization. After 1861 the *bureaux* only remained in the south.

4 During Ramadan, Muslims fast from dawn—when they can distinguish between a *white* thread (symbolizing light) and a *black* thread—until sunset, when they can no longer distinguish a white thread from a black thread.

5 Prostitutes named after the Oulad-Naïl region they hail from. For more see Maupassant's description further on in ch. VI, pp. 36 ff.

6 A name by which Muslims call Christians and, more broadly, Europeans. Perhaps to be translated as 'infidels'.

7 The Aissawa or Issawa are a mystical religious brotherhood that were founded in Meknès, Morocco, by the Sufi mystic Muhammad Ben Aïssâ (1465-1526). They are found predominantly in the Maghreb and are famed for their symbolic trance-inducing dances that they perform publicly during national and religious festivals.

8 From the nobility, of a noble house [lit. 'from a big tent'].

9 Fortified towns.

10 The Grand Mosque of Algiers, in the rue de la Marine, was built in 1097 by Youssef Ibn Tachfin (1009-1106), first king of the Berber Almoravide dynasty (r. 1061-1106). The minaret was built in 1324 by the Sultan of Tlemcen, Abu Tashufin of the Berber Abdalwadid dynasty (r. 1318-37). An outer gallery was added to the mosque in 1836.

11 A mufti interprets Qur'anic law and carries out religious, civil and judiciary functions.

12 As Maupassant says, the Casbah, or Kasbah, is the old quarter of certain North African towns that surrounds a castle or citadel.

13 *The Thousand and One Nights* or *Arabian Nights* are a collection of tales including 'Ali Baba' and 'Sinbad the Sailor' that had been related orally by Arab storytellers from the 10th century. They were supposed to have been told to the sultan by Scheherazade, his bride, who would start a tale and only agree to finish it the following evening, as a way of avoiding the sultan's habit of executing his wives following the wedding night to prevent their infidelity.

14 Lit. 'Stream of Monkeys Inn'. The hôtel du Ruisseau des Singes, Gorges de la Chiffa, Blida, is still open today.

Notes

[15] The decree of August 26, 1881 distinguished *communes de plein exercice*, with a strong European population, administered by an elected mayor, from *communes mixtes*, that were in the majority of a Muslim population, and entrusted to a civil administrator.

[16] Mozabites are people from the Mzab region of Saharan Algeria. See Maupassant's description later on in ch. VII, pp. 72-4.

[17] Socrates (c.469-399 BC), Athenian philosopher. Alcibiades (c. 450-404 BC), Athenian general. The possibility of a homosexual relationship between the two is discussed in Plato's *Symposium*.

[18] Gaius Julius Caesar (100-44 BC), Roman statesman and military leader. Suetonius (c. 69-c. 150 AD) implies a homosexual relationship between Caesar and Nicomedes IV, king of Bithynia (c. 94-74 BC), in his *The Twelve Caesars*. Cassius Dio, in his *Roman History*, has Caesar deny this.

[19] Henri III (1551-89), king of France from 1574. Henri was renowned for the effeminate manners and appearance of himself and his court favourites, known as Les Mignons, though the question of his sexuality has divided historians, some saying that accusations of homosexuality owe their origin to scabrous rumours spread by his enemies in the Catholic League.

[20] Denise Brahimi suggests, in her 'Présentation' to Guy de Maupassant, *Écrits sur le Maghreb* (Paris: Minerve, 1988), p. 17, that Maupassant's attack on homosexuality, perhaps unexpected from a man who was renowned as a libertine, was maybe to further emphasize his theme of difference between Arab and French culture, and perhaps also a way of sneaking in a couple of spicy anecdotes under the cover of fierce censure.

[21] The word here translated as 'Turkish baths' is, in the French, *hammam*. In the first edition Maupassant has this lower case in the first mention and with an initial capital in the second instance. Most later editions have emended the second to *hammam* (lower case), but it is possible that both should be upper case, Maupassant referring to a particular Parisian establishment. Cf. Maupassant, *Fort comme la mort*, ed. Daniel Mortier (Paris: Pocket, 1999), pp. 209-12, where Maupassant describes a visit to a *Hammam* in Paris which the editor Daniel Mortier says existed in reality, on the rue Auber.

[22] Maupassant is making a play on the word *tente* [tent] which is spelled and pronounced similarly to *tante* [lit. 'aunt'], a slang term for a homosexual, similar to 'fairy'.

[23] i.e., cross-legged.

Notes

Chapter Seven: The Zar'ez

1. The 'Bach'agha with the wooden leg' is Si Yahia Ben Hamoudi (1788-1884) who was also described by Émile Masqueray (1843-94), French anthropologist, in *Souvenirs et visions d'Afrique* (1894), ed. Michèle Salinas (Paris: La Boîte à Documents, 1989), p. 54. A bach'agha is superior to an agha (see ch. V n. 5), 'bach' coming from the Turkish word *bash* meaning 'head'.

2. The Creil pottery produced a British import similar to Wedgwood's Queen's Ware. Instead of the traditional hand-painted decorations, printed reproductions were used. It merged with the Montereau factory, closing in 1895, though products would continue to appear with the Creil-Montereau name until 1955.

3. Leben is a kind of sour milk or yoghurt.

4. A cadi or *qadi* is a minor judge in Muslim towns and villages that follow sharia (Islamic religious) law. The distinction between secular and religious life in Islam being blurred, *qadis* tend to preside over all legal matters involving Muslims.

5. *Pesos duros*, Spanish silver dollars widely used in Spanish colonies and elsewhere, worth 8 reales (hence their other name 'Pieces of eight'). The *peso duro* was equivalent to about 5 fr 19 centimes at Maupassant's time.

6. Muslims believe that each word of the Qur'an comes direct from God, some believing that the actual written word contains this divinity. As such, some wear amulets or carry about small leather pouches which contain scraps of paper upon which are written verses from the Qur'an, in particular the names of Allah. This is frowned upon by Islamic authorities, but the practice continues today.

7. Microbes were a recent discovery, the word *microbe* being coined by Charles-Emmanuel Sedillot (1804-83) in 1878 just three years before Maupassant was writing.

8. A *gandoura* is a short, loose, sleeveless garment.

9. *Sebkra* or *sebkha* is the Arabic word for a salt flat.

10. A léfaa is a horned viper (*cerastes cerastes gasperetii*), also known as the cerastes and the sand viper; it is a highly venomous snake which has a horny spine above each eye. It reaches about 85 cm in length.

11. A monitor lizard (genus: *veranus*)—the Arabic name, *ouran*, sounded like 'warnen' to the Germans which in English became the 'warning' and later the 'monitor' lizard.

12. Herodotus, *The Histories*, tr. Aubrey De Selincourt (Harmondsworth: Penguin Classics, 1954), Book IV, §192, p. 306: 'In the nomads' country [...] one finds [...] land-crocodiles like huge lizards, four and a half feet long'.

[13] Maupassant is perhaps referring to one of the species of snakes known as sand racers, renowned for their rapacity.

[14] The sand fish (*scincus scincus*) grows up to about 8 inches in length.

[15] One of the most illustrious restaurants in nineteenth-century Paris, located on the Boulevard des Italiens. The Café closed in 1913.

[16] The question of Maupassant's antisemitism is a difficult one to address and outside of *To the Sun* is most often brought up in association with his portrayal of Jewish characters in his novels *Bel-Ami* (1885) and *Mont-Oriol* (1887). In these novels there is a resentment of the power and wealth accumulated by Jewish bankers and businessmen in Paris and Maupassant may only be relaying an antisemitism that he saw was prevalent in the society he was portraying. Indeed antisemitic feelings were becoming increasingly prevalent in France in the 1880s. In 1881 a weekly paper was founded in Paris called *L'Anti-Juif* and later on in the decade the French journalist Édouard Drumont (1844-1917) would attack the roles of Jews in France, calling from their exclusion from society in his book *La France Juive* (1886) before going on to found the Antisemitic League of France in 1889. On one level, for Maupassant in *Bel-Ami* and *Mont-Oriol*, a certain respect can be seen for these influential Jewish financiers, '*une estime inquiète*' [an uneasy respect] (Henri Troyat, *Maupsassant* (Paris: Flammarion), p. 150, quoted in Guy de Maupassant, *Carnets de Voyage*, ed. Gérard Delaisement (Paris: Rive Droite, 2006), p. 453), in that, for example, the (partly autobiographical) hero of *Bel-Ami*, Georges Duroy, aspires to their status and standing in society, and this regard would be in accordance with what we expect of Maupassant, the 'industrialist of literature' (see my 'Introduction'). On the other hand, in *Mont-Oriol*, although the Jewish banker William Andermatt is perhaps the novel's most sympathetically read character—a loving husband and a doting father in a world of infidelities—he is also drawn in gross stereotypical terms. Like Monsieur Walter, the Jewish newspaper proprietor in *Bel-Ami*, Andermatt is viewed with contempt by the other characters, ridiculed, and cuckolded. Here in this passage of *To the Sun* is probably Maupassant's most explicit and unambiguous (and disgusting) pieces of antisemitic spleen. Even here he is strangely selective, making sure to distinguish between Jewish people of Europe and Algiers and those of the south of Algeria, and again between those Jews of the south of Algeria and the 'Jews of the desert', the Mozabites, whom he goes on to praise highly. Denise Brahimi says, in her 'Présentation' to Guy de Maupassant, *Écrits sur le Maghreb* (Paris: Minerve, 1988), pp. 18-20, that we should probably read this passage in context of

Maupassant's critique of Algeria's administration as a whole, and bear in mind Maupassant's suggestion that the powerful financial grip the Jews have over the Arabs stems from the French occupation. Brahimi goes on to say that perhaps Maupassant's invective against the Jews is part of a larger railing against the corruption predominant in Algeria and can be paralleled in his critique of the great native chiefs in ch. VIII. In his personal life, Maupassant was a regular frequenter of Jewish salons in Paris, having close relationships and love affairs with several Jewish women. The 'recent massacres' Maupassant speaks of are probably the wave of anti-Jewish pogroms that swept the south-western provinces of the Russian Empire after the assassination of Tsar Alexander II (1818-81, r. 1855-81) on March 1, 1881 (Old Style, March 13 New Style) when false rumours were spread that the assassins were Jewish. Millions of roubles of damages were done to Jewish property and there were numerous fatalaties in the pogroms at Elisavetgrad in the Ukranian province of Khersan on April 15, 1881 (April 27 New Style) and at Kiev on April 26 (May 7 New Style) and copycat violence spread across the region.

[17] The earliest religious sect of Islam whose origins stem from the disputes following the death of the third Caliph, in AD 656. Kharijism is often associated with fundamentalism and complete observance of the teachings of the Qur'an. The extremist element of Kharijism believed in the practice of *takfir*—that all unbelievers could be killed with impunity. Those who acted contrary to the Qur'an were expelled from Kharijite communities. Kharijism held the view that all believers, Arab and non-Arab alike, were equal, helping to gain converts from the Berber and Persian people. Kharijism itself splintered into various sects, one of which, the Ibadis, still exists today, with communities in Oman, the Mzab in Algeria, and Tunisia and Libya. In more recent times terrorist groups who stress the use of *takfir* are often branded as neo-Kharijites.

[18] The booklet Maupassant is referring to is A Cöyne, *Le Mzab*, an extract from the *Revue africaine* (Algiers: Adolphe Jourdan, Libraire-Éditeur, 1879). The quoted passage is from pp. 5-6.

[19] The five towns are: El-Ateuf, Bou-Noura, Melika, Beni-Isguen, and Ghardaïa.

[20] A *koubba* is a monument over a marabout's tomb.

[21] *La Commune de Paris* was the local authority which exercised control over Paris from March 18 to May 28, 1871. There was strong opposition in Paris to the official government headed by Adolphe Thiers in the wake of the French humiliation in the Franco-Prussian War and the agreement to allow the Prussians a symbolic victory

parade in the capital. The Parisian National Guard was still armed from the Siege of Paris (September 19, 1870-January 28, 1871) and had control of a large number of cannons. Thiers removed the government to Versailles, leaving a power vacuum that was filled by the Commune, which had 92 members, consisting of reformist republicans, various socialists, skilled workers and professionals. In the brief time the Commune was in power, reforms included: the separation of Church and state; the right to vote for women; pensions for the unmarried partners and children of National Guardsmen killed in service; and the remission of rents for the period of the Siege of Paris. Skirmishes between the regular army and the National Guard began on April 2 until fighting ended after a series of bloody encounters on May 28. Thousands of communards were killed in the resistance and many more were later executed.

[22] Besides the confederation of five towns mentioned in ch. VII n. 19 above, the other two towns of the Mzab are: Berrian, a day and a half's walk from Ghardaïa; and Guerara, 86 km east-north-east of El-Ateuf.

[23] Probably the 'Billard du colonel Pein' otherwise known as Qalat Dhiab, a mountain 18 km north-west of Bou-Saada. Named after the French soldier and explorer Louis Auguste Théodore Pein (1810-91), the Billard du colonel Pein sports Roman ruins upon its 743 m high summit.

Chapter Eight: Kabylie - Bougie

[1] See ch. VI, n. 1 above. The case for *Algérien* being in some sense a synonym for *colon* is even stronger in this instance.

[2] 'Viceroy' is not, here, a specific title, but another way of referring to the Governor-General of Algeria.

[3] Perhaps a reference to l'École d'administration which was created by the Minister of Education, Lazare Hippolyte Carnot (1801-88), in 1848 and established in the former building of the Collège du Pleissis in Paris. L'École d'administration was intended to train up future politicians and administrators and be a centre of political thought, however, it was short lived and closed the following year. Or maybe Maupassant is referring to l'École d'administration militaire which was established in 1875 at Vincennes only to be disbanded in 1879 and replaced the following year by three separate schools dedicated to infantry, cavalry and the engineer corps respectively. Albert Grévy (see also ch. II n. 7 above) was the first civil governor of Algeria and was the brother of Jules Grévy (1807-91), President of the French Third

Notes

Republic 1879-87.

⁴ As in the English, the French word *action*, which Maupassant uses, can have military connotations.

⁵ Sahraoui, agha of the Harrars (see ch. V n. 8).

⁶ On April 8, 1864, Lieutenant-Colonel Beauprêtre was massacred near Tiaret with all of his men (about one hundred) by the rebel leader Si Sliman and his men. Si Sliman also died in the attack.

⁷ The Agha of Frenda was the Si Ahmed Ould Kadi.

⁸ La porte sarrazine or Bab-El-Bahr is a stone archway that formed part of the old fortifications of Bejaïa. It was one of six gates (only two survive today) that date back to the reign of Nasir ibn Alnas (r. 1062-86), the fifth ruler of the Berber Hammadid dynasty.

⁹ In French, '*lanternes vénitiennes*', lit. 'Venetian lanterns'.

¹⁰ The Franco-Prussian War of 1870-1.

¹¹ Camille Regnault de Lannoy (1809-81)? See <http://www.alger-roi.net/Alger/villages/pages_liees/fghij/jemmapes_pn54.htm> where a list of the mayors of Jemmapes is given: Kayser, de Lannoy, Denis, Merle, before Ernest Perney became the village's first elected mayor in 1884.

¹² A *gourbi* is a shack or hovel.

Chapter Nine: Constantine

¹ Nuremberg trees are artificial Christmas trees made from goose feathers with their 'branches' spaced out to facilitate decoration. The Germans were particularly fond of decorating trees at Christmas, white pines being the favoured choice. In the latter part of the nineteenth century, this passion for the Christmas tree was so popular it caused concerns about deforestation and German legislation forbade the cutting down of real trees for festive decoration. The artificial Nuremberg trees, made in the style of white pines, could be from a few inches to a good few feet in height.

² Dante Alighieri (1265-1321), Italian poet. Maupassant's description of the Roumel alludes to Phlegethon, a river of boiling blood, one of the four rivers of hell in Dante's *Inferno*, Canto XII.

³ Mansourah is a hill north-east of Constantine and Sidi-Mecid is a ravine and waterfall near Constantine.

⁴ Biskris are people from Biskra; Mzabis or Mozabites are from the Mzab region in

Saharan Algeria; a *turco* is a native infantryman in the African army; *kadi* is an alternative spelling of cadi (see ch. VII n. 4).

⁵   Hadj Ahmed Bey (1784-1850) was the last bey of Constantine (r. 1826-48). Hadj Ahmed constructed his palace in Constantine from 1828-35. For details about the expropriations, demolitions and great costs involved in the building of the palace see Charles Féraud, *Visite au Palais de Constantine* (1877), which can be viewed online at <http://www.constantine.free.fr/LaVille/visiteaupalais>.

⁶   By 1185 all the Roman bridges were destroyed save the pont d'El Kantara which was restored in 1792 by Salah Bey (1725-92, r. 1771-92), stones being taken from the ruins of the Roman amphitheatre to restore its aqueduct. The bridge and aqueduct collapsed following the passage of a detachment of infantry in 1857. A new iron pont d'El Kantara was opened in 1863 and is 128 m long and stands 125 m above the Roumel.

⁷   A sister ship of the *Abd El Kader* (see ch. II n. 4), the *Kléber* was also built in 1880 for the Compagnie Générale Transatlantique, and was in service until 1901.

Fragments

At the Spas

¹   Loëche-les-Bains, also known as Leukerbad, is found in the Swiss canton of Valais. Maupassant travelled to Loëche for his health in August 1877.

²   A louis d'or was a gold coin worth twenty francs.

³   Le Conservatoire de Musique et de Déclamation, formerly the Ecole royale de chant, was founded in 1784. La salle du théâtre du Conservatoire, completed in 1811, was situated on the rue du Faubourg-Poissonniére.

⁴   In French '*le coupé*'—both the brougham (named after and designed for Henry Brougham (1778-1868), British politician, abolitionist, and Lord Chancellor of Great Britain 1830-4) and the coupé were light four-wheeled closed carriages that could be pulled by one, two or four horses. The driver would sit on a box seat outside at the front whilst inside would seat two (sometimes with an additional fold away seat).

⁵   Valais is a canton in southern Switzerland, also known as Wallis.

⁶   The Jungfrau (in German, translating as *jeune fille*, 'young girl' or *La Vierge*, 'the Virgin', in French) is a mountain 4158 m high in the Berner Oberland [Bernese Highlands] of the Swiss canton of Bern.

⁷   Thun is a town in the canton of Bern, on the shore of the Lake of Thun which is

situated at the foot of the Bernese Alps.

8 Mont Rose or Monte Rosa (4634 m) and Le Cervin or Matterhorn (4477 m) are mountains on the Italian border in the Swiss canton of Valais. La Dent-du-Midi (3257 m) is a mountain on the French border in the west of the Swiss canton of Valais.

9 The Gemmi Pass, some 2323 m high, links Loëche in the canton of Valais with the Berner Oberland. Halfway across the Pass is the Schwarenbach Inn where Maupassant set his story 'L'Auberge' ['The Inn'] (1886).

10 i.e., their titles are false, they are going under aliases.

11 The Odéon Theatre first opened in 1782, housing the French national theatre, the Comédie Française. It is situated near Les Jardins du Luxembourg in Paris.

12 The Torrenthorn, nicknamed 'Rigi [king] du Valais', is a mountain 2998 m high situated nearby to Loëche.

13 The Rhindenhorn or Rinderhütte, meaning 'cattle hut', is a mountain 2310 m high in Valais. Mont Blanc is the highest mountain in the Alps (4807 m) and is found on the French border with Italy.

14 Les Cassines or Cachines is a promenade in Florence on the banks of the Arno. Cassines are small (often white) country dwellings.

In Brittany

1 The *Collection des Guides-Joanne* were a series of nineteenth-century guidebooks to France published by Louis Hachette under the editorship of Adolphe Joanne (1813-81). They were similar to other European tourist guides, such as the Baedeker, and were the antecedent of the *Guide Bleu* in modern France. As Maupassant intimates, the *Guides-Joannes* were full of figures and statistics: exchange rates, distances, lists of stations, etc., and they set out daily itineraries for the reader, focusing on the railway as mode of transport. The 'excellent German guide' is probably the aforementioned Baedeker, from the German publishing house established by Karl Baedeker (1801-59) in 1827 that specialized in travel guides.

2 In French, '*la carte dite d'état-major*'.

3 Eugène Fromentin (1820-76), French painter and novelist who was one of the first French artists to depict Algeria in his work. His paintings are renowned for their vibrant use of colour. His literary works include *Dominique* (1863) and *Une Année dans le Sahel* (1858). He published *Un Été dans le Sahara*, the account of his travels in the Sahara, in 1857.

Notes

⁴ A tumulus is an artificially formed mound of earth covered in stones and concealing a burial chamber. Menhirs (from the Breton, meaning 'standing stone') are large upstanding megaliths, sometimes solitary, but often arranged in rows or circles. Dolmens (from the Breton, meaning 'long stone') are ancient burial chambers, structures resembling tables, built of large stone slabs which support another flat stone that forms a 'roof'. Most of these megaliths in Brittany were constructed from between 4500-200 BC.

⁵ The Château de Sucinio, a moated fortress built in the thirteenth century, lies near the town of Sarzeau in the Morbihan département of Brittany.

⁶ Arthur III, duc de Bretagne (1393-1458, duc from 1457), was an important figure in the Hundred Years War. He was named connétable de France by Charles VII in 1425. He fought under the banner of Joan of Arc at the Battle of Patay (1429) and was the major advisor behind the military reforms that turned Charles VII's army into a successful outfit. He recaptured Paris in 1436 and orchestrated the French victory at the Battle of Formigny (1450) which ensured the return of Normandy to France.

⁷ Pierre (or Peter) Abélard (1079-1142), French philosopher and theologian. He was very popular as a lecturer, using dialectical methods, and was the author of *Sic et non* (1121) which stressed the importance of looking at both sides of any issue. In spite of his influence and importance as an intellectual, he is now best remembered for his love affair with Héloïse (1101-1164), a French abbess. Abélard became abbot of the monastery of Saint-Gildas-de-Rhuys in Brittany in 1125.

⁸ A Chouan is a member of a peasant group of counter-revolutionary royalist insurgents in the Vendée area of west France who rose up from 1793-1800, named after one of their leaders, Jean Cottereau (1757-94) who was given the nickname of *chouan*, a Breton word meaning 'screech owl', because he rallied his troops in the night imitating the hoot of this bird. The Chouans objected to the republican government's policies on religion and enforced conscription. A Chouan was also used to describe those who rose in opposition to the July Revolution of 1830 when the last Bourbon monarch, Charles X was overthrown. A Chouan was, therefore, broadly speaking, a supporter of the older branch of the Bourbons. The gesture towards Quiberon invokes l'affaire de Quiberon of June 1795 when Général Hoche slaughtered the Chouans (and a force of emigrants supplied by the English) at Fort Penthièvre on the Quiberon peninsular.

⁹ Maupassant could be referring to La Table des Marchands (named after the Marchand family who owned the land, but sometimes erroneously referred to as the Merchant's Table), an engraved dolmen in Locmariaquer. Or perhaps La Chaise de César [Caesar's

Chair], a big menhir 2 metres tall in woods 2 km southeast of Erdevan. Or La Butte de César [Caesar's mound], also known as Tumiac, a tumulus in Arzon 15 m high and 260 m in circumference, so-called because it is believed that Julius Caesar used it as an observation post in his naval battles against the Vénètes (the inhabitants of the port of Vannes) in 56 BC.

[10] This story shares many elements in common with legends from other Celtic folklore, in particular with that of Taliesin the Bard from the Welsh collection, *The Mabinogion*, tr. Lady Charlotte Guest (London: Bernard Quaritch, 1877), pp. 471-6:

> In times past there lived in Penllyn a man of gentle lineage, named Tegid Voel, and his dwelling was in the midst of the lake Tegid, and his wife was called Caridwen. And there was born to him of his wife a son named Morvran ab Tegid, and also a daughter named Creirwy, the fairest maiden in the world was she; and they had a brother, the most ill-favoured man in the world, Avagddu. Now Caridwen his mother thought that he was not likely to be admitted among men of noble birth, by reason of his ugliness, unless he had some exalted merits or knowledge. For it was in the beginning of Arthur's time and of the Round Table.
>
> So she resolved, according to the arts of the books of the Fferyllt, to boil a cauldron of Inspiration and Science for her son, that his reception might be honourable because of his knowledge of the mysteries of the future state of the world.
>
> Then she began to boil the cauldron, which from the beginning of its boiling might not cease to boil for a year and a day, until three blessed drops were obtained of the grace of Inspiration.
>
> And she put Gwion Bach the son of Gwreang of Llanfair in Caereinion, in Powys, to stir the cauldron, and a blind man named Morda to kindle the fire beneath it, and she charged them that they should not suffer it to cease boiling for the space of a year and a day. And she herself, according to the books of the astronomers, and in planetary hours, gathered every day of all charm-bearing herbs. And one day, towards the end of the year, as Caridwen was culling plants and making incantations, it chanced that three drops of the charmed liquor flew out of the cauldron and fell upon the finger of Gwion Bach. And by reason of their great heat he put his finger to his mouth, and

the instant he put those marvel-working drops into his mouth, he foresaw everything that was to come, and perceived that his chief care must be to guard against the wiles of Caridwen, for vast was her skill. And in very great fear he fled towards his own land. And the cauldron burst in two, because all the liquor within it except the three charm-bearing drops was poisonous, so that the horses of Gwyddno Garanhir were poisoned by the water of the stream into which the liquor of the cauldron ran, and the confluence of that stream was called the Poison of the Horses of Gwyddno from that time forth.

Thereupon came in Caridwen and saw all the toil of the whole year lost. And she seized a billet of wood and struck the blind Morda on the head until one of his eyes fell out upon his cheek. And he said, 'Wrongfully hast thou disfigured me, for I am innocent. Thy loss was not because of me.' 'Thou speakest truth,' said Caridwen, 'it was Gwion Bach who robbed me.'

And she went forth after him, running. And he saw her, and changed himself into a hare and fled. But she changed herself into a greyhound and turned him. And he ran towards a river, and became a fish. And she in the form of an otter-bitch chased him under the water, until he was fain to turn himself into a bird of the air. She, as a hawk, followed him and gave him no rest in the sky. And just as she was about to stoop upon him, and he was in fear of death, he espied a heap of winnowed wheat on the floor of a barn, and he dropped among the wheat, and turned himself into one of the grains. Then she transformed herself into a high-crested black hen, and went to the wheat and scratched it with her feet, and found him out and swallowed him. And, as the story says, she bore him nine months, and when she was delivered of him, she could not find it in her heart to kill him, by reason of his beauty. So she wrapped him in a leathern bag, and cast him into the sea to the mercy of God, on the twenty-ninth day of April.

And at that time the weir of Gwyddno was on the strand between Dyvi and Aberystwyth, near to his own castle, and the value of an hundred pounds was taken in that weir every May eve. And in those days Gwyddno had an only son named Elphin, the most hapless of youths, and the most needy. And it grieved his father sore, for he thought that he was born in an evil hour. And by the advice of his council, his father had granted him the drawing of the weir that year, to see if good luck would ever befall him, and to give him something wherewith to begin the world.

And the next day when Elphin went to look, there was nothing in the weir. But as he turned back he perceived the leathern bag upon a pole of the weir. Then said one of the weir-ward unto Elphin, 'Thou wast never unlucky until to-night, and now thou hast destroyed the virtues of the weir, which always yielded the value of an hundred pounds every May eve, and to-night there is nothing but this leathern skin within it.' 'How now,' said Elphin, 'there may be therein the value of an hundred pounds.' Well, they took up the leathern bag, and he who opened it saw the forehead of the boy, and said to Elphin, 'Behold a radiant brow!'

'Taliesin be he called,' said Elphin. And he lifted the boy in his arms, and lamenting his mischance, he placed him sorrowfully behind him. And he made his horse amble gently, that before had been trotting, and he carried him as softly as if he had been sitting in the easiest chair in the world. And presently the boy made a Consolation and praise to Elphin, and foretold honour to Elphin[.]

Taliesin was a historical Welsh poet of the sixth century, believed to have been a court bard to kings of Powys and Rheged.

[11] There was a castle in Pont-l'Abbé in the middle of the tenth century, built on the grounds of the Abbey of Loctudy; the present Château des Barons du Pont dates back to the thirteenth century and although it was set on fire by protesting peasants in 1675, it was rebuilt at the beginning of the eighteenth century. Today the Château houses the town hall and the Bigouden Museum.

[12] The River Odet.

[13] The old Penmarch lighthouse dates from 1835, but ceased to be used in 1897 when the new electric Phare d'Eckmül was opened just a couple of hundred yards away. The old lighthouse still stands and today houses the Centre de Découverte maritime.

[14] In French a *lame* or *vague sourde* seems to be a particular piece of marine terminology meaning '[une] lame qui s'élève sans qu'on ait senti le vent qui l'a soulevée' [a wave which rises without one having felt the wind which got it up], *Grand Larousse encyclopédique*, 10 vols. (Paris: Librairie Larousse, 1960-4), vol. 9, p. 936. I have struggled to find an equivalent technical phrase in English.

Notes

[15] On October 10, 1870, the préfet du Morbihan, Gustave Levainville, was having a picnic on the rock with his family. Whilst the préfet climbed up higher to go and speak with an archaeologist, Duchatelier, a child cried out 'A wave, a wave', but by the time the préfet had turned around there was no one left on the rock. His wife, daughter and three other family members had been carried away and it took all the witnesses and onlookers to stop the préfet from throwing himself in the sea after them. The rock, commemorated by a cross, continues to attract visitors and, unfortunately, victims. A 25-year-old photographer, taking pictures of the sea, was swept away by a wave in 1997.

[16] Possibly the calvary at La chappelle de Notre Dame de Tronoen near Saint Guénolé, one of the oldest calvaries in Brittany dating back to c. 1450. It is made of a rectangular base with two friezes (including a representation of the Nativity) upon which stand the three crosses of the crucifixion of Christ and the two thiefs, all carved in granite.

[17] Although violets are edible, having a sweet taste as well as a sweet fragrance, I think Maupassant's analogy is to the violet's association with modesty, its flower being hidden away amongst its leaves.

[18] Victor Hugo (1802-85), 'Océano Nox' (w. July 1836) from *Les Rayons et les ombres* (1840). The quoted lines are taken from the final stanza:

> *Où sont-ils, les marins sombrés dans les nuits noires ?*
> *O flots ! que vous savez de lugubres histoires !*
> *Flots profonds redoutés des mères à genoux !*
> *Vous vous les racontez en montant les marées,*
> *Et c'est ce qui vous fait ces voix désespérées*
> *Que vous avez le soir, quand vous venez vers nous !*

> [Where are they, the sailors sunk in the black of night?
> Oh the waves! I bet you know some gloomy stories!
> Deep waves ever dreaded by mothers on their knees!
> You recount them to yourself when you raise your tide,
> And it's this that gives you those desparate voices
> You have in the evening when you come towards us!]

[19] The two lighthouses are most likely the phare du Bec du Raz, built in 1826 and 18 m high and the feu de la falaise du Raz, a metal turret constructed in 1870, both of

which were extinguished in 1887 with the opening of the phare de la Vielle. The phare de la Vielle is probably the lighthouse Maupassant says 'they have tried to complete for ten years'—it was first commissioned in 1861, but lack of finances meant the project was adjourned for ten years. Technical difficulties then meant that it wasn't until 1879 that preliminary work could begin, and it was in 1882 that construction proper got underway.

[20] The traditional verse about the Breton coast runs as follows:

Qui voit Molène voit sa peine, qui voit Ouessant voit son sang,
qui voit Sein voit sa fin, mais qui voit Groix voit sa joie

[He who sees Molène sees his own pain, he who sees Ouessant sees his own blood,
he who sees Sein sees his own end, but he who sees Groix sees his joy]

[21] Le Trou de l'Enfer is in actual fact found among the rocks of Saint Guénolé, near Penmarch, not on la Pointe du Raz. There is also a spectacular chasm on the Ile de Groix known as Le Trou de l'Enfer.

[22] A similar Breton canticle, 'Ann Ifern' [Hell], features in Th. de la Villemarqué, *Barzaz-Breiz. Chants populaires de la Bretagne*, 2 vols. (Paris: Delloye, 1839-40), vol. II, pt. 3, no. iv, pp. 348-53, where the Breton is given a facing page French translation which appears below:

L'Enfer

Descendons tous, chrétiens, en enfer, pour voir quels tourments affreux et épouvantables endurent les âmes damnées que la colère de Dieu tient enchaînées au milieu des flammes, parce qu'elles se sont éloignées de lui en ce monde.

L'enfer est un abîme plein de ténèbres, où ne luit jamais la plus petite clarté; les portes ont été fermées et verrouillées par Dieu, et il ne les ouvrira jamais; la clef en est perdue!

Les dalles rougies d'un four d'ici-bas ne sont que fumée, au prix du feu qui dévore les âmes damnées en enfer; mieux vaudrait brûler, en ce four, jusqu'à la fin du monde, que d'être, pendant une heure, tourmenté en enfer.

Ils hurlent à tue-tête, comme des chiens enragés; ils ne savent où fuir; partout des flammes! des flammes sur leur tête, des flammes sous leurs pieds, des flammes de tous côtés, qui les dévoreront à jamais.
Le fils s'élancera sur son père, et la fille sur sa mère, et les traîneront par les cheveux, au milieu des flammes, avec mille malédictions:
—Soyez maudite, femme perdue, qui nous avez mis au monde; soyez maudit, homme insouciant, qui êtes la cause de notre damnation!—

Ce sera satan qui leur préparera à manger, et les ordures des monstres de l'enfer, ramassés dans les ruisseaux de feu, qu'il leu servira; et pour boisson, ils auront leurs larmes, mêlées de mille immondices et de sang de crapauds.
Et leur peau sera écorchée, et leur chair déchirée par la dent des serpents et des démons; et leur chair et leurs os seront jetés au feu, pour alimenter la fournaise immense de l'enfer.

Après qu'ils auront été laissés quelque temps dans les flammes, ils seront plongés, par satan, dans un lac de glace; et du lac de glace replongés dans les flammes, et des flammes dans l'eau, comme la barre de fer en forge.

Alors, ils se mettront à pleurer, à pleurer amèrement:
—Ayez pitié, mon Dieu, ayez pitié de nous!—
Mais ce sera en vain qu'ils pleureront, car tant que Dieu durera, dureront leurs tourments et leurs maux.

Le feu qui les brûlera en enfer sera si vif, que leur moelle bouillîra dans leurs os; plus ils demanderont grâce, plus ils seront tourmentés; ils auront beau hurler, ils brûleront éternellement.

Ce feu-là, c'est la colère de Dieu qui l'a allumé; et il ne pourrait plus l'éteindre, quand même il le voudrait; jamais il ne jettera de fumée, et jamais il ne consumera; il les brûlera éternellement, sans jamais les détruire.

[Hell

Notes

Let us descend, Christians, to hell, to see what awful and appalling torments endure the souls of the damned that the anger of God holds enchained in the midst of flames because they were so distant from him in the world.

Hell is an abyss full of shadows where not a slither of light ever shines; the doors have been closed and bolted by God, and he will never open them, the key to them is lost!

The reddened flagstones of a furnace here on earth are but smoke compared to the fire which devours the damned souls in hell; it would be better to burn in such a furnace till the end of the world than to be tormented in hell for just one hour.

They scream their heads off like rabid dogs; they don't know where to flee; everywhere flames! flames over their heads, flames under their feet, flames on all sides which will devour them forever.
The son will hurl himself at his father, and the daughter at her mother, and they will drag them by the hair into the middle of the flames with a thousand cusses:
— Curse you, lost woman, who brought us into the world; Be cursed, insouciant man, who is the cause of our damnation!—

It'll be satan who'll prepare something for them to eat, and the filth of the monsters of hell, collected from streams of fire, will be what he serves them; and for a drink they will have their tears mixed with much excrement and the blood of toads.
And their skin will be scorched and their flesh ripped off by the teeth of serpents and demons; and their flesh and bones will be thrown into the fire to feed the great furnace of hell.

After they have been left for a while in the flames, satan will plunge them into a lake of ice; and from the lake of ice they will be plunged once more into the flames, and from the flames into the water, like a bar of iron in a forge.

And so they begin to cry, to cry bitterly:

—Have pity, my God, have pity on us!—

But it'll be in vain that they cry, for as long as God exists, so too will their torments and their ills exist.

The fire that will burn them in hell will be so intense that their marrow will boil in their bones; the more they ask for grace the more will they be tormented; shout all they want, they will burn eternally.

It's the wrath of God that lights the fire there; and he can no longer extinguish it even if he'd like to; the smoke will never clear and [the fire] will never burn out; it will burn them eternally without ever destroying them.]

[23] This is the Étang de Laoual.

[24] Ys or Is was the capital of the historical Cornouaille region of Brittany. It is said that it was built below sea level and protected by dykes and was so prosperous that Paris was named after it (*par-Is*, 'like Is'). The legend of the drowned city of Ys has several variations, but most, like Maupassant's version, centre around the same characters: King Gradlon (possibly to be equated with King Gradlon Mawr of Brittany (c. 330-434)), his daughter, Dahut, and Saint Guenolé or Winwaloe (d. 532), the founder of the abbey of Landévennec. In other variations, at the command of the Black Prince (who is none other than the devil) with whom she has fallen in love, Dahut steals the gold or silver key to the floodgates that her father wears around his neck and opens the gates, flooding the city.

Le Creusot

[1] Le Creusot is in the Saône-et-Loire département (no. 71) in the Bourgogne region of France.

[2] Montchanin is a town just south of le Creusot.

[3] Joseph Eugène Schneider (1805-75) and his brother Adolphe Schneider (1802-45) took over the running of the le Creusot forges in 1836; they were originally founded by François Ignace de Wendel (1741-95) and William Wilkinson (1743-1808) in 1782.

[4] Henry Bessemer (1813-98), an English engineer who invented a new converter for the manufacture of steel in 1855.

Appendix—Place Names in *To the Sun*

Place name in *To the Sun*	Currently known as
Aïn-Cherchar	Aïn Charchar
Aïn-el-Hadjar	Aïn-el-Hadjar
Aïn-Kétifa	El Ketifa
Aïn-Sfisifa	Sfissifa
Algiers	Alger
Attia	Attia
Aumale	Sour El Ghozlane
Bas-Yala	Ras-el-Ma ?
Beni-Amram	Beni-Amran ?
Beni-Foughal	Beni-Foughal (a tribal area)
Beni-Isguem	Beni-Isguen
Beni-Mansour	Beni-Mansour
Besson	Zitouna / Bessonbourg
Biskra	Biskra
Boghar	Boghar
Bône	Annaba
Bordj-el-Hammam	Aïn el-Hammam
Bougie	Bejaïa
Boukhrari	Ksar El Boukhari
Bou-Saada	Bou-Saada
Cavalho	El Aouana
Chabet / Chabet-el-Akhra	Chabet-El-Akra

Chélif (river, valley)	Chéliff
Chellala	Chellala Dahrania
Chiffa (river, gorges, town)	Chiffa
Collo	Collo
Constantine	Constantine
Damrémont	Damrémont / Hammadi Krouma
Dayat-Kereb	Dayet-El-Kerch ?
Djebel-Amour (mountains)	Djebel-Amour
Djebel-Gada (mountains)	?
Djebel-Nefoussa	Jebel Nefoussa
Djelfa	Djelfa
le Djendel	Djendel
Djidjelli	Jijel
Djurjura (mountain)	Djurjura
El-Arrouch	El-Arrouch / El Harrouch
El-Ghedir	El Ghedir
El-Maya	El-May
El-Milia	El Milia
l'Estaya	Estaya ? (forest, hill, near Collo)
Fendeck	Oued Fendeck
Fil-Fila	Filfila
Frenda	Frenda
Gastu	Zit Emba
Géryville	El Bayadh
Haci-Tirsine	Tircine
Hazabra	Ouled Hbaba ?
Hodna (plain, chott)	Chott El Hodna
Jemmapes	Azzaba
Kabylie (region)	Kabylie
Kerrata	Kherrata
Khang-el-Melah (mountain)	Rocher de Sel (near river Oued El-Melah)
Kralfallah	Khalfallah
le Kreïder	Kreïder
Ksar-el-Krelifa / Ksar-Krelifa	Sidi Khalifa

Appendix—Place Names

Laghouat	Laghouat
Mansoura (hill)	Mansourah
Marhoum	Marhoum
Médéah	Médéa
Mezrech	Sidi Mezghich ?
Mitidja (plain)	Mitidja
Mograr	Moghrar
Msila	M'sila
Mustapha	Mustapha
Mzab (region)	Mzab
Oran	Oran
Orléansville	Chlef
Oued-Deb (river)	Oued Deb
Oued-Fallette (river)	Oued Falette
Oued-Goudi (river)	Oued Goudi
Oued-Mzab (river)	Oued M'zab
Oued-Roumel (river)	Oued Rhumel
Oued Saïda (river)	Oued Saïda
Oulad-Mokhtar	Oulad Mokhtar
Oulad-Naïl (mountains)	Oulad-Naïl
Philippeville	Skikda
poste de la Fontaine	Aïn el-Hammam
Raïane Chergui	?
Rezaïna	Rezaïna
Robertville	Em Jez Ed Chich
Roumel (river)	Rhumel
Ruisseau-des-Singes	Ruisseau des Singes
Sahel (river, valley)	Oued Sahel
Saïda	Saïda
Saint-Antoine	El Hedaick
Saint-Charles	Ramdane Djamel
Sétif	Sétif
Sidi-Meçid (ravine, waterfall)	Sidi-Mecid
Stora	Stora

To the Sun

Tafraoua	Tafraoua
Tis-Moulins	Tismouline
Trafi	Et Trafi
Valée	Hamoudi Hamrouche
Zar'ez / Zar'ez-Chergui (chott)	Zahrez Chergui
Zeramna	Forêt Domaniale du Zeramna
Zériban	Zeriba

Index

Abd-el-Kader, 18
Abd-el-Kader (ship), 9
Abd-el-Kader-bel-Hout, 53
Abélard, Pierre, 108
abyss, 88, 99, 114; *see also* chasm
Africa(n), 6, 10, 12, 15, 16, 17, 23, 34, 37, 40, 46, 56, 58, 70, 72, 90; North Africa, 72
agha(s), 24, 60, 71, 78, 79, 80, 81
Aïn-Cherchar, 85
Aïn-el-Hadjar, 19, 20
Aïn-Kétifa, 24, 25
Aïn-Sfisifa, 25
Aïssaouas, 30
Alcibiades, 40
Algeria(n), 7, 10, 12, 13, 20, 24, 26, 31, 35, 40, 70, 71, 72, 73, 75, 76, 77, 78, 80, 82, 85, 88, 106; *see also* Arab(s)
Algérien(s), 29, 75
Algiers, 10, 11-13, 15, 26, 29, 56, 70, 82, 90, 91; European quarter, 11, 12; Grand Mosque, 31; skating rink, 12
Allah, 15, 51; *see also* God
Alps, the, 97, 99, 100, 102
Alsace, 19; Alsatian, 19
Amar-ben-Habilès, 87

ant lion, 64
Arab(s), 7, 11, 12, 13, 20, 22, 23, 25, 26, 27, 28, 29, 30, 31, 32, 33, 34, 35, 36, 38, 39, 40, 41, 43, 44, 45, 47, 48, 49, 50, 51, 52, 53, 54, 55, 56, 57, 58, 61, 62, 63, 64, 65, 66, 68, 69, 70, 71, 72, 73, 76, 77, 78, 79, 80, 81, 86, 87, 88, 89, 90, 91; Arabic, 12, 65, 72, 83, 90; *see also* Algeria(n)
Aravik-Du, 109
army, 10, 17, 23, 28, 46, 66, 71, 84; arms, 76; *see also* military
Arnault, Pol, 3
Arthur III, duc de Bretagne, *see* Richemont, *connétable* de,
Assyrian, 37
Atlantic Ocean, 113; Ocean, 106, 107, 108, 112, 113, 119
Atlas mountains, 17, 33, 77
Attia, 85
Auberge du *Ruisseau-des-Singes*, 33, 34
Audierne, 113; la baie d', 113
Aumale, 75
Austria, 100

bach'agha(s), 45, 46, 71, 78, 81
Baedeker, 105

baie des Trépassés, 118
Barbary, 72
bassin de la Joliette, le, 9
Basle, 96, 97
Bas-Yala, 27
Beauprêtre, Colonel, 80
Belad-el-Haoua, 89
Beni-Amram, 86
Beni-Foughal, 87
Beni-Isguem, 74
Beni-Mansour, 82
Beni-Mzab, 72; see also Mozabite(s); Mzab
Berne, 97
Bessemer, Henry, 122, 124
Bessin (concession), 85
Besson, 86
'Billiard Table', the, 74
Bisern, M., 86
Biskra, 80; Biskris, 90
Boghar, 31, 35, 42, 43, 44, 52
Bône, 91
bone(s), 21, 34, 51, 53, 67, 98, 116, 117; see also carcass
Bordj-el-Hammam, 57
Bou-Abdallah, 43
Bou-Amama, 7, 16, 17, 23, 24, 25, 26, 27, 46, 76, 79
Bougie, 75, 82; gulf of, 83
Boukhrari, 33, 34, 35, 36, 42, 43, 45
Bou-Saada, 29, 43, 57, 63, 68, 69, 70, 71, 74
Brest, 114, 120
Breton(s), 106, 108, 110, 115; see also Brittany
bridges, 91
Bringeard, Brigadier, 24
Brittany, 105, 106, 107, 110; see also Breton(s)
Brunetière, 25
Bullier (Bal), 13
bureaux arabes, 29, 30, 43, 78, 80, 81

cadi, 51, 52; kadis, 90
Caesar, 40, 108
Café Anglais, 64
caïd(s), 24, 29, 45, 46, 47, 48, 50, 51, 53, 56, 58, 65, 71, 81, 82, 87; see also chief(s)
camels, 20, 21, 25, 27, 44, 48, 50, 66, 67, 68, 71, 73, 80, 90
carcass, 20, 34, 68; see also bone(s)
Carnac, 107, 108
Carpentier, Édouard, 86
Carthaginian hens, 20
Casbah, 32
Cassines, 103
Catholic, 32
Cavalho, 86
cemeteries, 41, 49
Cérez, General, 25
Cervin, le, 99
Chabet, 89
Chabet-el-Akhra, 84
Chamber, the, 76
chasm, 89, 91, 99, 102, 114; see also abyss
Chebka, 72, 73
Chélif, 15, 34, 44
Chellala, 24
chief(s), 24, 25, 27, 54, 58, 65, 71, 76, 78, 79, 80, 81, 82; see also caïd(s)
Chiffa gorge, 33
chott(s), 20, 21, 25, 27
Chouan, 108
Christ, 120
civil, (administrator), 35, (party), 79, (servants), 82; civilian, 17, 29; civilization, 12, 40, 49, 71, 73, 79, 82; civilized, 30; civilizing, 81
cloud(s), 15, 16, 21, 44, 54, 55, 59, 67, 71, 82, 84, 91, 102, 107, 108, 121, 124
Collo, 85, 86
colonist(s), 19, 26, 76, 77, 81, 84, 88;

colonization, 12, 23, 76, 79, 80, 88; colonized, 15; colonizers, 7; colony, 10, 15, 30, 71, 77, 78, 80, 88
commune mixte, 35, 36, 85
commune de plein exercise, 35, 36
Commune (Paris), 73
Conquet, 112
Conservatoire, the, 96, 101
Constantine, 89-91
Corsicans, 9
couscous, 31, 50, 55, 60, 64, 70
Coÿne, Commander, 72, 74
Creil, 49
Creiz-Viou, 109
Creusot, le, 121, 124

Damrémont, 85, 86
dam(s), 10, 17, 69, 73, 76, 77; Habra, 17
Dante, 89
Dayat-Kereb, 26
Dellis, 44
Dent-du-Midi, la, 99
Department of Civil Engineering, 10
desert, 6, 7, 10, 21, 26, 29, 31, 35, 36, 43, 44, 47, 56, 60, 62, 63, 64, 66, 69, 70, 72, 73, 76, 78, 80, 81, 91, 106, 107; deserted, 21, 67, 107
Deshoulières, Mme, 7
Détrie, General, 25
Djebel-Amour, 48, 70
Djebel-Gada, 46, 53, 56, 57
Djebel-Nefoussa, 72
Djelfa, 43, 56, 66, 80; agha of, 60, 80
Djendel, le, 85
Djidjelli, 86
Djurjura, 75
Domingo, 26
Douarnenez, 106, 107, 118, 120
Druids, 108, 109, 111; Druidic, 106
douar(s), 16, 53, 55, 85

earth, 13, 15, 16, 21, 34, 35, 39, 42, 44, 45, 46, 49, 51, 53, 54, 55, 59, 66, 67, 69, 82, 89, 110, 111; *see also* soil
Egyptian, 38
El-Akhedar-ben-Yahia, 45
El-Arrouch, 85
El-Ghedir, 85
El-Haoués-ben-Yahia, 45
El-Maya, 25
El-Milia, 86
l'Enfer, 114
engineer(s), 10, 20, 77; Department of Civil Engineering, 10
English, 9, 48, 107; Englishman, 113
English Channel, 113
Eskimos, 49
esparto, 20, 21, 23, 46, 50, 56, 58, 61
l'Estaya, 86
Europe(ans), 11, 12, 15, 16, 28, 39, 49, 56, 70, 72, 74, 75, 76, 77, 81, 82, 88, 113

famine, 23
fanatics, fanatacism, *see* religious fanaticism
farmers, farming, 15, 23, 46, 67, 76, 86; farms, 80, 85; *see also* esparto; sheep
Fendeck, 86
Fil-Fila, 86
fire, 7, 10, 19, 21, 34, 36, 37, 47, 50, 54, 61, 69, 74, 82-7, 115, 116, 117, 121, 122, 123, 124
Flaubert, Gustave, 7
Florence, 103
forests, forestry, 21, 34, 60, 69, 75, 77, 82, 84, 85, 86, 87, 88, 101; *see also* woods
France, 22, 29, 30, 34, 36, 39, 40, 47, 75, 76, 82, 84, 89, 91, 106, 107, 120; French, 9, 11, 12, 13, 16, 17, 18, 24, 27, 31, 35, 36, 39, 41, 42, 46, 52, 53, 57, 66, 71, 74, 76, 78,

79, 80, 81, 83, 88, 111, 118
Franco-Algerian Company, 20, 24
Franco-Prussian War, 19, 84
Frenda (agha of), 80
Fromentin, Eugene, 106; *Un Été dans le Sahara*, 106

Gastu, 85
gazelle, 70
Gemmi Pass, 99
Geneva, 103
German, 84, 105
Géryville, 24, 25
glaciers, 97, 98, 99, 100, 102
God, 51, 52, 53, 102, 106, 109, 116, 117, 119; goddesses, 42; *see also* Allah
goums, 24, 25, 79; *goumiers*, 22
Gouydno, King, 110
government, 10 (military), 26, 77, 78, 81, 85, 87, 88; governed, 35, 76; governing, 77, 78; governor, 10, 25, 77, 78, 87; governs, 53, 123
Greece, 6; Greeks, 9, 40
Grévy, Albert, 10, 78
Gwiou, 109, 110

Habra dam, 17
Haci-Tirsine, 24, 25
Hadj-Ahmed, 90; palace of, 90
Hammada, 72
hammam, *see* steam room; Turkish baths
Harrars, 24
Hassassenas, 24
hauts plateaux, 16, 17, 18, 20, 23, 46
Hazabra, 85
heat, 6, 9, 16, 17, 19, 21, 28, 30, 34, 36, 45, 48, 53, 54, 60, 64, 66, 68, 72, 76, 91, 97, 98, 123; hot, 18, 34, 50, 58, 82, 87
hell, 89, 114, 115-18, 121

Henri III, 40
Herodotus, 62
Hodna, 57
horizon, 6, 10, 15, 16, 20, 21, 29, 30, 34, 36, 44, 45, 46, 54, 55, 56, 57, 58, 59, 60, 66, 68, 69, 82, 84, 99, 100, 102, 105, 107, 112, 114
horned viper, *see léfaa*
horse(s), 9, 16, 27, 28, 44, 45, 46, 48, 49, 51, 54, 56, 59, 60, 61, 64, 68, 71, 80, 82, 84, 90, 119; horsemen, 16, 20, 21, 25, 26, 27, 28, 41, 43, 44, 45, 47, 48, 49, 56, 61, 65
Hu, 109, 110
Hungary, 100; Hungarians, 17
hurricane, 55, 64, 82; *see also* sandstorms
hyenas, 18, 66, 84
L'Hyène, 20

Indies, the, 6
Innocenti, Colonel, 24
iron, 16, 34, 49, 84, 91, 110, 121, 122, 123, 124
Israel, 71
Italy, 100; Italians, 9, 74

jackal, 18, 20, 53, 66, 67, 68, 84
Jacquet, Commander, 27
Japan, 6; Japanese, 49
Jemmapes, 85
Jews, 32, 70, 71, 72; Jewish women, 90
Joanne (Guide), 105
Jungfrau, 97, 102
justice, 51, 52; Justice of the Peace, 52

Kabyle(s), 12, 75, 76, 77, 82, 84, 85, 90; Kabylie, 15, 75, 76, 77, 82
Kerrata, 85
Khang-el-Melah, 66
Kléber, 91
Koridwen, 109, 110

Index

korrigan(s), 109, 110
Kralfallah, 21, 25
Kharijism, 72
Kreïder, le, 24, 25, 27
Ksar-el-Krelifa, 25, 27
ksar(s), 33, 35, 36, 46, 70

Laghouat, 29, 33, 63, 72, 106
Lapps, 49
law, 23, 30, 41, 71, 76, 77, 87; lawsuit, 51, 52
Leconte de Lisle, 6
léfaa, 61-3, 70
Lefebvre (concession), 85
Legion of Honour, 65
Lesseps (concession), 85
Levat (concession), 85
light, 6, 11, 16, 32, 38, 47, 58, 82, 83, 106, 107, 109, 112, 114, 116, 120
lion, 66
lizards, 18, 62, 63, 64, 66; see also ouran
Locmariaker, 107, 108
Loëche, 95-101
Lorient, 110
Lovenberg, 100

mad (treatment of), 57-8
Malbranque, Steed, 163
Mallaret, 25, 27
Maltese, 9
Mansoura, 89
marabouts, 15, 24, 25, 27, 30, 31, 32
Marhoum, 27
Marseille, 9, 10; Marseillais, 9
Mary, see Virgin Mary
meadow, 99, 125
Mecca, 31
Médéah, 33, 34
Mediterranean, 84, 91
Mezrech, 87
Midi, le, 36, 62
military, 10, 24, 26, 27, 29, 35, 36, 76, 79, 80, 81; see also army
mirage, 21, 59, 65, 68
Mitidja (plain of), 15, 29, 33, 77
moeurs, 12, 13, 30, 39, 40, 41, 46, 64, 77, 105
Mogrars, 25
Mohammed, 30; Mohammedan, 30, 52; the Prophet, 72,
Mont Blanc, 102
Montchanin, 121
moors, 106, 107, 108, 110, 111, 113
Moorish, 37, 39, 45, 83, 90
morality, morals, see moeurs
Morbihan, 106, 107, 110, 112
Morda, 109
Moroccan, 78
Mor-Vrau, 109
mosques, 11, 48, 70; Grand Mosque of Algiers, 31
mount(ains), 11, 15, 17, 18, 19, 20, 32, 33, 34, 35, 37, 44, 45, 46, 49, 51, 56, 58, 59, 66, 68, 69, 74, 75, 76, 77, 83, 84, 97, 98, 100, 102, 106, 114, 122, 124
Mozabite(s), 37, 70, 72, 73, 74; see also Beni-Mzab; Mzab
Msila, 57
mufti, 31, 32
Muslim(s), 7, 51, 52, 72; see also Mohammedan
Mustapha, 13
Mzab, 70, 72, 73; Oued, 73; Mzabis, 90; see also Beni-Mzab; Mozabite(s)

Nanterre, 16
Napoléon III, 13
negroes, 9, 12, 36, 38, 39, 40, 49, 90; negress, 19
Neuilly, 13
nomads, 16, 36, 47, 75; nomadic, 40, 65
Norman, 67

North, the, 28, 35, 36, 55; Northern, 44, 48
North Africa, 72
Nuremberg, 89

oasis, 68, 70, 106; oases, 30, 39, 74; *see also* rivers; sources; streams; water; wells
ocean, 10, 21, 23, 59, 64, 66, 106, 107, 108, 112, 113, 114, 118, 119; *see also* sea
Odéon, the, 101
Oran, 15, 16
Ordnance Survey, 105
Oriental, 18, 42, 65, 90
Orléansville, 16
Oued-Deb, 85
Oued-Fallette, 21, 22
Oued-Goudi, 85
Oued-Mzab, 73
Oued-Roumel, *see* Roumel, the
Oued Saïda, 18
Ouessant, île d', 114
Oulad-Alane, 52; Oulad-Alane-Berchieh, 45
Oulad-Dia, 65
Oulad-Messaoud, 85
Oulad-Mokhtar, 53
Oulad-Naïl, 30, 36-9, 40, 42, 45
ouran, 62, 63; *see also* lizards

Paris, 6, 40, 48, 77, 101, 103, 120; Parisian, 12, 13, 49; Commune of, 73
Pas-de-Calais, 15
Pélisaire, Blas Rojo, 26-7
Penmarch, 107, 111, 112
Philippeville, 85
Piedmont, 100, 102; Piedmontese Alps, 99
places militaires, 33
pointe du Raz, la, 107, 110, 113, 118

Pont-l'Abbé, 107, 110
Port-Navalo, 108
poste de la Fontaine, 57
poverty, 23, 34, 76, 77; poor, 9, 12, 19, 22, 34, 35, 43, 52, 53, 56, 58, 62, 66, 69, 74, 75, 95, 104
Prussian, 32
pyramids, 7, 98, 99

Quiberon, 108
Quimper, 110, 111, 120
Quimperlé, 110

Raïane Chergui, 63
railways, 15, 16, 21, 27, 120, 122, 124; *see also* trains
Ramadan, 7, 30, 31, 32, 43, 45
religious fanaticism, 23, 30, 32, 33
Rezaïna, 21
Rhindenhorn, the, 102
Rhône valley, 99, 100, 103
Richemont, *connétable* de, 107
Ripeyre, 86
rivers, 17, 18, 27, 33, 45, 59, 69, 74, 89, 91, 109, 110, 113, 116, 123; *see also* oasis; sources; streams; water; wells
Robertville, 86
Roman(s), 40, 74, 83, 89, 91
Rose, mont, 99
Roumel, the, 89, 91
Rueil, 16
rugs, 11, 18, 32, 39, 41, 47, 48, 54, 58, 64, 65, 70

Sahara(n), 35, 36, 56, 57, 62, 63, 69, 72, 74, 106
Sahel, 73
Saïda, 16, 17, 18, 22, 24, 25, 29; (agha of), 24, 79; (Oued), 18
Saint-Antoine, 85
Saint-Charles, 85
Saint-Gildas, 108

sand, 6, 7, 13, 21, 34, 46, 47, 55, 56, 58, 59, 60, 61, 62, 64, 65, 66, 67, 68, 69, 70, 84, 113, 118; dunes, 59, 60, 61, 63, 64, 65, 66, 84
sand fish, 63-4
sandstorms, 54-6, 82; see also hurricane
salt, 50, 57, 58, 59, 60, 64, 66, 112, 113
Saracen, 83
Satan, 119
Scheherazade, Sultana, 32
Schneider, Joseph Eugène and Adolphe, 121
scorpions, 21, 30, 39, 55, 61, 62, 66, 70
sea, 7, 9, 10, 11, 21, 30, 46, 59, 64, 82, 83, 84, 97, 105, 106, 107, 109, 111, 112, 113, 114, 116, 118, 119, 120; see also ocean
Sebkra, 57, 58, 59, 60
Sein, île de, 114
Seine, the, 7, 105
Sétif, 89
Sharrouï, 25, 79, 80
sheep, 16, 50, 65, 66, 71, 80, 81, 99, 111; mutton, 46, 50, 55, 60, 64; see also farmers
ships, 6, 10, 86, 112, 113, 118, 122, 123; Abd-el-Kader, 9; Kléber, 91; boats, 9, 10, 83, 113
Si Cherif-ben-Vhabeizzi, 65
Sider (concession), 85
Sidi-Meçid, 89
sirocco, 20, 21, 54
sky, 6, 10, 15, 19, 23, 33, 34, 35, 44, 46, 50, 54, 58, 59, 68, 69, 82, 83, 91, 98, 100, 102, 107, 109, 111, 121, 124
snakes, 30, 61, 62, 63, 84, 89, 124; serpents, 18, 61, 63, 121, 124; see also léfaa
snow, 11, 58, 59, 97, 98, 100, 102
Socrates, 40
Sodom, 40, 120

soil, 13, 15, 16, 19, 28, 34, 35, 46, 49, 59, 66, 67, 68, 72, 89, 107; see also earth
sources, 43, 45, 53, 69; see also oasis; rivers; streams; water; wells
South, the, 16, 21, 24, 29, 31, 35, 36, 43, 53, 64, 70, 71, 72, 80, 81
Southern Mail, 36
spahi(s), 29, 31, 41, 43, 44, 55, 62, 68, 90
Spanish, 9, 16, 17, 20, 21, 23, 24, 25, 26, 27, 63, 74
Sphinx, the, 7, 38
stars, 10, 30, 37, 47, 54, 58, 66, 70, 90
Stora, 85
steam room, 36, 39, 60, 122; see also Turkish baths
streams, 16, 18, 34, 70, 100, 123, 125; see also oasis; rivers; sources; water; wells
Sucinio (château of), 107
Sud-Oranais, 46
sun, 6, 9, 11, 15, 17, 21, 30, 31, 34, 35, 36, 42, 44, 46, 47, 48, 54, 55, 56, 57, 58, 59, 60, 64, 65, 66, 67, 68, 69, 70, 73, 74, 85, 90, 91, 97, 98, 99, 100, 101, 102, 105, 108, 109, 111, 118, 121
Sweden, 6
Switzerland, 98; Swiss, 33
Syria, 72

Tafraoua, 20, 25
tarantulas, 62, 70
Tartarin, 11
Teissier (concession), 85
telegraph, 10, 21, 24, 25, 26, 84
Tell, the, 19, 35, 77, 78, 81
Teur, 11; see also Turks
Thousand and One Nights, The, 32, 90
Thun, 98; (lake of), 98
Tis-Moulins, 27

toads, 62, 66, 100
Torrenthorn, the, 101
Trafis, 24, 79; Trafi, 27
trains, 6, 15, 16, 17, 20, 21, 24, 27, 48, 55, 103, 121, 124; *see also* railways
travel, 6, 29, 68, 96, 106; traveller(s), 29, 33, 48, 57, 58, 68, 73, 90, 105
tribes, 21, 22, 24, 25, 27, 30, 35, 39, 43, 47, 49, 51, 52, 53, 56, 58, 71, 72, 78, 79, 80, 81, 82, 87
Tripoli, 72
Tunisia, 19; Tunisian, 78
turcos, 90
Turks, 9, 11; Turkish, 7; baths, 40

Valais, 96
Valée, 85, 86
Vannes, 106, 107, 108
Vanoris, 100, 101, 102, 103
Vierge, la, 97
Virgin Mary, 113
vultures, 20, 21, 34, 68

water, 6, 10, 16, 17, 18, 19, 20, 21, 31, 33, 34, 43, 45, 48, 49, 50, 53, 54, 55, 57, 58, 59, 60, 66, 69, 73, 76, 77, 84, 85, 91, 100, 105, 106, 107, 108, 109, 110, 112, 114, 116, 118, 119, 120, 123, 125; *see also* oasis; rivers; sources; streams; wells
Weinbrenner, Lieutenant, 24
wells, 43, 45, 53, 54, 66, 67, 85, 100
wilderness, 7, 44, 57, 66, 67, 68, 106, 113
wind, 20, 34, 49, 54, 55, 62, 65, 69, 86, 87, 102, 106, 107, 108, 110, 111, 114, 115; *see also* sirocco
wolf, 111
woods, 7, 18, 33, 34, 60, 83, 84, 95, 86, 87, 98, 105; *see also* forests

Yahia-ben-Aïssa, 45
Ys, 119

Zar'ez, 43, 57, 58, 59; Zar'ez-Chergui, 57
Zeramna, 86
Zériban, 85
zouaves, 21, 86

Forthcoming from Duchy of Lambeth

The Foreign Soul *and* The Angelus

by
Guy de Maupassant

translated and edited by James Wilson

The first complete translation into English of Maupassant's two unfinished novels *L'Ame étrangère* and *L'Angélus* together with full critical apparatus. Published: Autumn, 2008.

www.ingramcontent.com/pod-product-compliance
Ingram Content Group UK Ltd.
Pitfield, Milton Keynes, MK11 3LW, UK
UKHW041450180426
11946UKWH00013B/147/J